MAKING
LITTLE BOXES
FROM WOOD

The author's mark.

Timber Samples

Box: Padouk.
Lid: English Oak, Quartered.
Inlay: Snakewood.
Bottom: Rosewood.

MAKING
LITTLE BOXES
FROM WOOD

JOHN BENNETT

GUILD OF MASTER CRAFTSMAN PUBLICATIONS LTD

First published 1993 by
Guild of Master Craftsman Publications Ltd,
166 High Street, Lewes, East Sussex BN7 1XU

Reprinted 1995

© John Bennett 1993

ISBN 0 946819 39 4

Illustrations © John Bennett 1993

Photographs © John Bennett 1993

Designed by Ian Hunt Design

Printed and bound in Great Britain by
Eyre & Spottiswoode Ltd

$\boxed{A}$

ACKNOWLEDGEMENTS

Throughout my woodworking life I have much for which to be thankful, especially so to individuals over the last 35 years. I was fortunate to come under the influence of A. W. P. Kettless during my sixth-form years of Advanced level GCE study. I regarded it as even more fortunate that he went to Shoreditch Training College as a lecturer, at the same time as I went as a student teacher; so to him, a much-respected craftsman, the 'Chippie with the Oxford accent', I owe a great deal.

As for this book, I have to say thank you to a few particular individuals. First, to Eddie Moore, a fellow woodwork teacher, who, like me, is now retired from active service, for his friendship, encouragement and constructive criticism. He checked my work and made many valuable comments on the manuscript. Second, to Elizabeth Inman, my editor at GMC Publications, for her help and guidance and for giving answers to my many inane questions; and to her assistant, Ian Kearey, for his work on the production of this book.

Many others, especially suppliers, have willingly given of their time and expertise.

My wife Brenda needs a special mention, if only because of all the hassle that she has had to put up with over the years! Things like sawdust and shavings carried into the house on shoes, odd pieces of wood decorating the house, questions such as 'Can you think of any more ideas?' and 'Where have you moved that bit of paper to?' – etc., etc!

To all who have helped, a very big 'Thank you'.

This book is dedicated to Brenda, my wife, and to Chay, Paul and Kirstie, my three grown-up offspring.

FOREWORD

by Alonzo Kettless FIOC, MGCI, NDD, FTC, C & G

When I was invited to write a foreword to this book, my thoughts immediately and happily flashed back to those years when I was teaching technical subjects at Taunton's School, Southampton. This school had a reputation second to none in craft and technical subjects, and John Bennett was a student there, during which time he studied for the advanced level in technical subjects.

While he was a pupil at the school I was awarded the first prize and a Diploma for advanced craftsmanship by the Worshipful Company of Carpenters, London. These were awarded for an intricate framed linenfold panel, which with the kind permission of the Carpenters Company I was able to display in the school's showcase. John Bennett was very impressed, and spent hours studying the panel and its construction!

His book, *Making Little Boxes from Wood*, amply illustrates his dedication to working in wood. He has researched into the history and development of little boxes, and each box is introduced, and is accompanied by a photograph, clear instructions, diagrams and a cutting list.

The work has been carefully planned to cater for the beginner, and advances to more complex construction and decorative features to satisfy the more competent craftsman. This book should assist teachers of CDT in schools, while the more experienced woodworker is encouraged to develop his or her own ideas.

These little boxes are most useful and a delight to behold, which makes this book a must for all lovers of wood. A knowledge of timber and its properties is of paramount importance to the woodworker, therefore why not celebrate and make a worthy little box to hold your specimens of this wonderful material – then you really will have boxed a collection of wood! I am very pleased to recommend this delightful and informative book, and to wish it every success.

C

CONTENTS

1

INTRODUCTION

Over the years, boxes and containers become important objects in life, so much so that we even end our days in a box! Many containers are purely functional, whilst others are decorative to a high degree.

My dictionary defines a box as 'a receptacle or container made of wood, cardboard, etc., usually rectangular and having a removable or hinged lid.' Fortunately, this does not mean that all boxes and containers have to be rectangular. We are constantly reminded that 'variety is the spice of life', and this must also be true of craftsmen: how boring it would be to produce boxes that were all of the same size and shape! Fortunately, using timber, no two boxes can ever be the same (unless something like MDF is used, especially with a photographic veneer applied to its surface).

Probably the best-known antique boxes are writing slopes and tea caddies. The latter were made for the few wealthy people who could afford to buy the new beverage to have come from across the seas. These caddies were richly decorated with exotic veneers from far around the world, and many now command very high prices in auctions and antique shops. Writing slopes were also decorated with veneer and sometimes with an inlay of brass, cut into very intricate shapes.

It is well worth the effort to visit musical museums, such as the one at Chichester, Sussex, to study the beautiful boxes that were produced to house musical movements of various kinds. The woodworking skills displayed are exquisite, as indeed are the varieties of timber used. Where no musical museum exists, take the trouble to look around antique shops for these objects as well as for other boxes. The prices will probably frighten you, but just stop and think for a moment; your boxes could one day appear in such shops – but you might not be around to see it happen! As a general observation, I feel that all craftsmen who are pleased with their work should in some way sign it or mark with a stamp. Too often in the past this has not been done, and now no record exists of many craftsmen and their work.

In Victorian and early Edwardian times, glove boxes were introduced in order that ladies' gloves could be neatly stored without being folded. Jewellery has also been kept in boxes, as well as pencils, spices, tools, equipment of various kinds, money and many other items. The list is endless.

As far as making boxes is concerned, there is a tremendous amount of satisfaction to be derived in making a box or container. The use is less important than the making in many instances. They become very individual, even to some extent when the design is copied, if only because the timber will be different. To see what I mean, try making two identical boxes from very different timbers. Boxes can be made simply, sometimes very quickly, and generally from a small amount of timber. They make individual, distinctive and unique presents. The skill level needed is not necessarily high, provided you stick to the more simple joints. However, the more difficult joints, when cut properly, give the craftsman a great deal of personal satisfaction.

Most of the work described in this work requires only simple hand tools. Some processes are made considerably easier with the use of more advanced tools, but they are by no means obligatory.

In most of the designs, the type of joint used is unimportant. Very few boxes require the strength that a dovetail joint provides; however, it would be very boring to make all boxes using a mitre joint! Variation in joints will provide more interest. Select a joint that you are happy with and which will suit the intended use.

There are several boxes included where no specific measurements are recommended, because so much will depend on your requirements and the material available; suggested cutting lists are still provided, to show what was originally used. Do not follow designs slavishly, but instead use your own imagination and modify.

Beginners can start with the simple ideas and progress as far as they are able or want to go. For these people, I suggest that you use a different joint as soon as you have become reasonably happy and competent with a more simple construction. In this way you will progress in a systematic manner. More experienced woodworkers can use the book as a resource book for ideas.

By far the most important thing is to enjoy your box making; develop it to your own satisfaction, and gain a great sense of pleasure in using a beautiful and natural material in the making of objects of beauty.

Happy box making!

1

MATERIALS

The quality of the basic material is of prime importance in any type of work. In the case of a craftsman in wood, the raw material is varied and plentiful. The quality is sadly also variable, but good suppliers are to be found in most areas. Wood is the only naturally renewable material on the earth, but unless it is managed properly in a sustainable way it will not be able to regenerate at a sufficiently fast level.

TIMBER

There are over 70,000 different species of woods in the world, but of these less than 500 are available commercially. Most felled timber is used in its immediate locality, and so much is not exported. Many trees are quite small even when fully grown; the commercial conversion of these would result in astronomical costs, and would therefore be out of the question.

However, much valuable timber is burnt to provide extra land for agriculture in its many forms, and this land is rarely re-afforested. Many homeowners cut and burn small trees from their gardens which could provide beautiful timbers for the box maker. Lilac is one such tree, as it is frequently cut down and disposed of because the owner is fed up with the many suckers! The timber from this tree is hard and truly beautiful, with its splashes of lilac colouring. It needs care in seasoning, but as most of the wood will be small in size, this is no great problem provided that the process is not hurried.

Over the years I have specialized in the use of English timbers. There is a wide variety of colour, texture, grain, workability, beauty and availability. I do use imported timbers from all around the world, but I try to make sure that they come from a sustainable source. This does not mean that other timbers are not used, because some of my timber has been salvaged from old and badly broken furniture, or I have had it in stock for many years. It therefore follows that much of my stock would not now be regarded as coming from a renewable source.

Good quality timber in itself does not ensure good work, but it certainly helps! A good craftsman will get the best from any material, but a poor worker will not have the ability to get the best from his or her material. The choice of timber for a project is important, especially when different types are used in the same project. Timber chosen should be suitable for:

▪ the project
▪ its ultimate location
▪ the ability of the worker
▪ when more than one type is used in the same project, complementing the other timbers.

There are now areas of Papua New Guinea, the Solomon Islands and Peru where the forests are managed on a sustainable basis. These countries export timbers such as the spectacularly red-coloured chacahuante, amboyna and sonokeling (also known as Indonesian rosewood), chontaquiro, planchonia (red bombway), pencil cedar and kwila, to name but a few. Very few companies are exclusively providing material from renewable sources, but others do stock some varieties. These, together with our British home-grown varieties, provide us with a wide choice of interesting timbers. The big problem in box making is being able to buy small quantities of any one variety; co-operative buying provides a solution for many people.

Some timbers are more suitable than others for the woodworker, especially when making relatively small items such as boxes, as some timbers need a great deal of care in their use. Dermatitis can be a problem for some people when using certain timbers, while others can create breathing problems as well as throat and nasal irritation.

A story is told of a church that needed new pews; the congregation was persuaded by their amateur woodworking clergyman to order them in mansonia. He eventually found a company who would make them, but after a few hours of work, most of the employees went home with breathing problems. The company soon pulled out of the contract, and so others were approached.

The day finally arrived when they were complete and installed, at a much greater cost than was originally thought. Everything was fine until a couple of years later, when an obnoxious smell was noticed, especially after services and on warm days. It was finally established that the parishioners' shuffling on the pews had removed the polish and was acting like abrasive on the bare timber! The pews were removed and replaced with a traditional oak variety, at great expense.

It is now known that the dust from some timbers is carcinogenic, and the wood should only be worked with adequate and correct breathing apparatus. The motto must always be: check up on what you use.

English oak has a very open grain and does not often lend itself to small piece use. It is heavy but very beautiful, especially when quarter-cut. To get a smooth finish, it is better to fill the grain prior to polishing.

Yew is classified botanically as a softwood, but is harder than many hardwoods! It is a very beautiful timber, but can be extremely difficult to work. When the grain is straight, workability is good; however, when it is at its best visually, the grain is very wild and consequently difficult to work. The sapwood is a pale cream colour, and contrasts vividly with the various reds that can be found in its heartwood. Strictly speaking, the sapwood should not be used, because it contains all the food on which woodboring insects thrive, but it *is* used, and can be very striking in its contrast.

Douglas fir, or British Columbian pine, as the foreign variety is known, is another softwood which can be used for box making. It always has a 'clean' look about it , and often displays a beautiful grain pattern. A good sawmill will stock this timber, even down to 100mm × 9mm, and most will sell it in quite short lengths.

Ash, like oak, tends to be open-grained, but is very useful, especially in veneer form.

Beech tends to be very plain and lacking in character, unless it is quarter-cut, when it displays the rays as shimmering specks.

Plane is similar to beech, but really stands head and shoulders above most other timbers when quarter-cut. The rays are nothing short of spectacular, and because the wood is close-grained and hard, it takes a superb polish. This timber really is noble in its beauty.

Walnut has long been described as the best for furniture making, and was especially noted for its use around the Queen Anne period. Two varieties are available, each quite different in many ways: American black and English are both eminently suitable for our purposes, but do be prepared to pay a considerable amount for timber, especially good quality English!

Lilac has already been mentioned, and will probably not be available commercially, but is well worth the trouble of finding when cut down in gardens.

Laburnum unfortunately also fits into this category, although it is sometimes available in small sections. Both laburnum and yew have been used in the past as oyster veneer for drawer fronts and table tops. This method uses small branches which are cross-cut into thin pieces, edge-shaped and joined together as veneer. The resulting pattern is a mosaic of annual rings, a technique which could be used for boxes.

Fruit trees provide excellent timber, with **pear** having the most plain grain pattern. They are all hard and take an excellent finish.

Cedar is botanically a softwood that actually is soft in texture. However, it has a most beautiful aroma, and is therefore ideal for the linings of some boxes.

Sycamore is especially beautiful when quarter-cut, and displays a beautiful ray figure. Sometimes this figure is rippled and shows as ripple marks at right angles to the grain structure. This figure is very highly prized for violin backs and veneer, and is therefore very difficult to obtain in the solid.

Holly is regarded as the whitest known timber. It has a featureless grain and can take on a stain in the drying process, unless seasoned properly. It takes dye very well, and when dyed black, is often used as a substitute for ebony.

The range of foreign timbers is wide, and full descriptions can be found for all native and imported timbers in the many specialist books available from good bookshops.

Some timbers are available as 'spalted'. Spalting is caused by a fungus that attacks the wood when it is felled and left in contact with the soil. It has to be arrested before the fungus does too good a job and allows rotting to take place. It shows up generally as thin black lines that weave their way through the timber. This often makes an uninteresting and dull timber come alive and take on a new character. It is much sought after, and is becoming quite expensive as a result.

VENEER

Mankind has been using veneer for over 3000 years. It was probably introduced to the United Kingdom from the continent in the form of walnut, to cover home-grown timber such as oak.

Veneer is frequently suggested as a suitable material in the project section of this book, so what is it? In its simplest form, it is a very thin slice of wood, cut from the trunk, burr or roots of a tree. There are many ways in which this is done, and a great deal has been written in specialized books about the subject.

Originally veneer was sawn, but very little is now cut in this way, most being produced using a large knife in some way. In simple terms, a log is turned over a knife blade several feet long. As the veneer is peeled away from the log, the knife is moved closer into the log so that a continuous length of veneer is produced. On the more highly specialized cuts, such as quarter-cut, and also on exotic timbers, part of a log is made to reciprocate over a knife blade, so producing smaller sheets of veneer.

Sawn veneer is about 3mm thick, and therefore, because of this and the fact that saws waste a great deal of timber, it is very expensive. Modern knife-cut veneer is generally about 0.6mm thick, although for special purposes it is sometimes much thinner.

Veneer enables a very economical use of wood: a mature mahogany might produce about 450 cubic feet of usable timber, which is only about 7500ft of 4in × 2in board. Turned into veneer, the same tree would yield about 200,000 square feet. I am not suggesting that all timber should be converted to veneer, but it certainly makes a great deal of sense for the rarer timbers to be so treated.

The range of veneer is very extensive, and there are many companies that provide excellent service (see the List of Suppliers). However, as with solid timber, it does pay to select your own. A third party can only select what he or she hopes and thinks you want, and this might not be your best option!

GLUES

Since the end of the Second World War, there has been an explosion of new glues on to the market. The range available to the public is enormous, many of the glues being made for one purpose only. It is important to use the correct glue for the job in hand, and that means read the manufacturer's instructions and follow them exactly.

I well remember a boy at school several years ago, who needed to use a contact adhesive. As usual, I talked to him about what the glue was and how it had to be used, and finished by telling him to read the manufacturer's instructions. I left him to get on with the job while I helped other pupils. When I returned to him, he complained that the glue was not working. It transpired that he did not believe that the two surfaces had to be touch dry before being brought together!

The most useful type of glue for box making is polyvinyl acetate, or PVA. It is sold as a thick white liquid in a plastic container and is ready for use.

Although newer types set more quickly than their predecessors, most require the joint to be cramped for a short period. The glue cures totally in about 12 hours, but this is partially dependant on temperature and humidity. When used in a butt-joint type of application, the parts can drift apart when cramped; this can be overcome by spreading the glue, aligning the parts without cramps, separating them and then re-positioning with cramps. A word of warning – all PVA glues are useless if frosted, so store them in the warm.

Aliphatic glues are a more recent introduction, and are also white. They tend to drip and run less than PVA, and are also water- and heat-resistant. The 'grab' time is also an advantage, as cramping can be reduced.

The traditional glue for veneer work is old-fashioned animal glue. The smell is an acquired taste, as older craftsmen will testify! I only use this type when I am veneering a box in some way, and not when I am making up my own plywood. It has to be made up in a glue kettle and used hot. The advantage comes when laying veneer, as the glue can be softened by the heat of a domestic iron and the veneer can therefore be manoeuvred into its correct position. It does, however, have two major drawbacks: it can only be used hot, and it is not heat- or water-resistant.

In recent years a hot-melt glue in sheet form has been brought on to the market. In this material, the glue film is bonded on to a sheet of paper, from which it can be released. A domestic iron is used to provide the heat necessary, and so no cramping is needed. The big bonus is that it is ready to use, and every square inch can be used.

Urea formaldehyde glues are water- and heat-resistant, and require an acid hardener to activate the glue. Two types are available, the first with the hardener pre-mixed, requiring the addition of water to mix and activate, and the second as a two-part package where the resin is in powder form to be mixed to a paste with water and the hardener is supplied as a separate liquid. In the latter case, the resin paste is painted on to one surface and the hardener applied to the other. When the two are brought together, the hardening process begins.

The superglues, or cyanoacrylate adhesives, can be very useful in woodworking. They must be used with great caution, as they bond fingers just as well as wood! To avoid this danger, it is wise to use disposable gloves. These glues' use is probably best restricted to small repair work, such as when a small splinter has been broken off. In general, they bond in a very short time and work better when the parts fit together very well.

Hot-melt glue guns are of no, or very little, use in box making.

ABRASIVES

PAPERS

The choice of abrasive papers is now much wider than ever before. Standard glasspaper has been improved upon with the introduction of garnet paper: this is more expensive, but it outlasts the traditional paper in normal use. In recent years, aluminium oxide-coated papers have been introduced; I find that these are infinitely better than either traditional papers or garnet paper. Again, they tend to be more expensive, but the extra cost is small when compared with the lasting qualities and the finish obtained on the wood.

When using abrasive papers, it is important to begin with a coarse grit paper and then to work through the grades to produce a fine finish. There is no benefit to be gained by beginning with too fine a paper: you will use up far too much, as well as exerting too much energy, and will still not get very far! The object is to remove the marks and scratches that the previous paper has left behind, until a smooth surface is achieved. To this end, a range of 80, 120, 150, 180, 240 and 300 grit sizes will suffice. 400 grit is also useful for rubbing down polishes between coats.

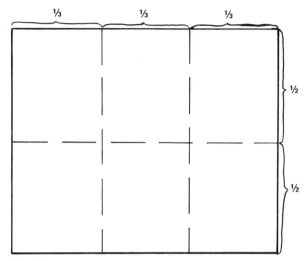

Fig 1.1 Cutting glasspaper.

Always use abrasive papers wrapped around a glasspaper block. This ensures that the edges remain sharp, and also distributes the weight evenly over a wider area. A standard block measures 110mm × 60mm × 30mm, and is made of cork. I buy a cork block, cut it in half through its thickness and mount the two pieces on to wood, which gives two blocks for little more than the price of one. A block of this size needs a sheet of glasspaper to be cut into six equally-sized pieces as shown in Fig 1.1; when cut in this way, little is wasted. As these papers tend to roll up when they get warm and dry, make a box to store them in. Chapter 6 shows one idea for this.

STEEL WOOL

This material is very useful in the polishing stages of work. You are likely only to need 0000 grade for this purpose. WARNING: despite the fact that this material is steel, it is very inflammable and must not be placed in a flame.

POLISHES

There is a great range of polishes available freely in hardware stores. In general, there is rarely a time when it can be said that a particular polish is the only one that can be used for a specific purpose. As the range is so great, one can only experiment with selected polishes, and use the ones that you, as an individual, favour.

Sanding sealer is based on one of two bases: spirit, or one of the chemicals similar to acetone. The second type is very noxious, and must never be used in an unventilated area. Both are applied with a cotton cloth and rubbed down between coats. Ideally, other preparations need to be applied as a final surface.

RUSTIN'S CLEAR PLASTIC COATING

This polish is superb, but does need a little care in its application. Two chemicals are mixed together in proportion and are then brushed on to the timber. It gives a very hard and glossy surface, although a matt or satin finish can also be produced. Use in a well-ventilated area and not near naked lights. Follow the manufacturer's instructions that are supplied with each pack.

OILS

There are many types of drying oils used for polish.

Danish oil produces a hard surface that will give only a sheen on timber. It is applied with a cloth, and each coat is left to dry before the next is applied. Final burnishing with a soft cloth will produce the final sheen.

Teak oil and **tung oil** are two further types, both of which are used in the same way as Danish oil.

Linseed oil has tended to lose favour in recent years, but it still gives a good finish, although the smell does linger!

OILS FOR FOOD

Where food is to come into contact with timber, use either **olive oil** or **peanut oil**.

WAX POLISH

Wax polish should only be applied on to a sealed timber surface. Good quality wax is applied by cloth and left for at least an hour so that its solvent can evaporate. The wax is then burnished with a soft, lint-free cloth.

Do not be tempted to use spray wax polishes, as many of these contain silicone, for which there is no solvent. Should you need to repolish a surface that has had this treatment, problems will arise, to the extent that the surface will need to be planed off below the level to which the silicone has penetrated.

HARDWARE

Good quality fittings are becoming harder to find. Solid drawn brass hinges are easily available in large sizes, but the smaller ones needed for boxes can be very difficult to obtain. Some are so poorly made that the opposite sides are different in size and even shape!

Chinese hinges are now available, and these are good in quality. Find a 'Fixings and Fastenings' retailer in Yellow Pages for this type of hardware.

When fixing hardware with brass screws, first drive in a steel screw of the same size and thread pattern, and then replace it with the brass screw. This ensures that the soft head of a brass screw is not spoilt when driven in. I prefer to align the slots in the screw heads in the same direction, because I feel that a better appearance is achieved. This may be a controversial idea, but it is nevertheless a technique that I always use.

Small locks are also difficult to find in any variety, and suggestions for finding these are made at the end of the book. Ceramic magnets, however, make a good alternative, and can be obtained as small circular plates which can be let and glued into a surface.

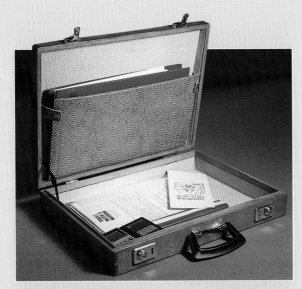

Briefcase: vitex and pomele mahogany veneer.

'Celebration of wood': padouk, English oak, rosewood, snakewood, American black walnut and red gum.

Student's stationery compendium: steamed pear and ebony veneer.

Pentagonal box: chacahuante and walnut.

Glasspaper container: pine, and router cutter box: yew and sycamore.

Jewellery box: American walnut and sycamore.
Triangular boxes: American walnut and Australian silky oak.

Spice boxes: steamed pear and holly, and tea caddy: figured sycamore and chacahuante.

Paper tissue box cover: yew, telephone noteblock holder: cedar, and magazine slipcase: pine and birch ply.

Potpourri box: walnut and ash, and musical box: quartered plane, sycamore and cedar.

Eye box: ash and rosewood, heart box: teak, circular box: Australian silky oak and walnut, and elliptical box: walnut and teak.

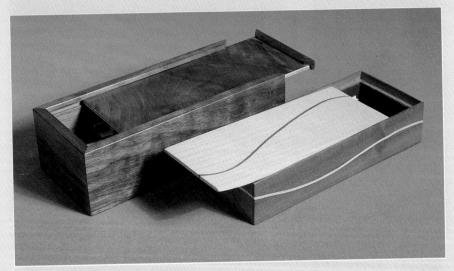

Traditional pencil box: American black walnut and English walnut, and desk pencil box: planchonia and ash.

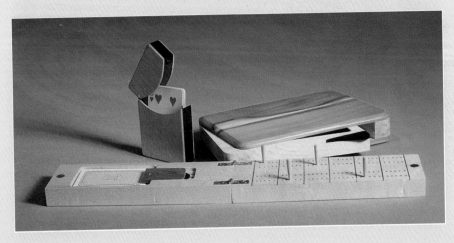

Single card box: ebony and English oak, swivel box: yew and sycamore; card box and crib board: sycamore, mahogany and lilac.

$$\boxed{2}$$

TOOLS

Very few tools will be needed to make boxes, and most will be already found in a standard toolbox. Over the years, personal experience has led me to favouring a particular type of tool, but I emphasize that this is individual preference only. You will undoubtedly find the same for each craftsman in any trade.

GOLDEN RULES

1 Read up all you can in specialist books on each tool that you intend to use.
2 Remember that tools should be treated with a great deal of tender loving care, and should therefore never be abused.
3 Always keep *all* parts of your body behind cutting edges.
4 Edge tools should always be kept sharp. If you cut yourself, try to do it with a sharp tool, as this will cut cleanly and not tear! The resultant cut will heal much more quickly.
5 If you use power tools, learn how to use them safely. Seek advice *and* training from a competent craftsman.

PLANES

A **bench plane** is essential for planing timber to size. Ideally, a jack plane and a smoothing plane would be the minimum requirement, but either

Fig 2.1 From left to right: smoothing plane, block plane and shoulder plane.

would suffice on its own (*see* Fig 2.1). A small **block plane,** preferably with an adjustable mouth, makes life easy when planing end grain and also for working small chamfers. As you will need to work grooves and rebates, a small **plough plane** will be needed, unless you have access to a portable electric router. A plough plane is generally only used for grooving, but it can double as a rebate plane and therefore comes cheaper than two planes.

SAWS

Back saws are essential for any bench work, especially so for box making. I use a **tenon saw** for general purpose work and a **dovetail saw** for fine work, and have recently been favouring a **Japanese back saw** for fine work (*see* Fig 2.2). This saw cuts on the pull stroke and therefore takes some getting used to, as Western saws cut on the push stroke. It is very fine and is ideally suited for delicate work. The other difference is that the handle is straight rather than hand-grip shape. A **coping saw** will enable you to cut curves and remove waste from dovetail joints. When cutting with a saw, remember that a saw removes waste, and therefore the golden rule must be: 'Always cut on the waste side of the line.'

CHISELS

I deplore the feel of plastic-handled chisels and try only to buy the wooden-handled varieties (*see* Fig 2.3). The old craftsmen used to buy chisels unhandled, and then turned up different shaped handles for each chisel so that they could recognize a particular size by the shape and wood of the handle. I still feel that this is a good idea.

Of the modern chisels, I have a couple of Japanese chisels that I favour almost to the exclusion of all others. These chisels are short, and have socket tangs which are fixed to red oak handles that are hooped at the end. The major difference from Western chisels is that the blade is made of laminated steel and has been hollow ground on the back. The laminations produce a very hard steel which retains its edge beautifully. The back needs to be polished like a mirror by successive rubbing on progressively finer oil- or water stones, and the hollow grinding enables very fine cuts to be made.

All chisels and planes will be improved in performance if their blade backs are polished in this way. It does take a little time to achieve, but the effort is well rewarded by the improvement in the cutting quality of the tool. I find that 3mm,

Fig 2.2 From top to bottom: Japanese *ikedame* saw, tenon saw and dovetail saw.

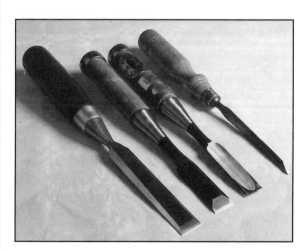

Fig 2.3 From left to right: socket bevel-edged chisel, two Japanese bevel-edged chisels (note the hollow-ground back) and 3mm bevel-edged chisel.

Fig 2.4 Top left to right: cutting gauge and two marking gauges. Below top to bottom: sliding bevel, marking knife and engineer's square.

4.5mm, 6mm, 9mm and 12mm chisels are needed for most eventualities. Very occasionally I have needed a chisel smaller than 3mm, and so have modified a 3mm to suit. All of these chisels need to be of the bevel-edged variety, especially when dovetailing.

MARKING TOOLS

A **pencil**, **knife**, **try square** and **marking gauge** are basic equipment (*see* Fig 2.4). Choose a pencil which is not too soft, and definitely not a carpenter's pencil, as this will give a line about a mile wide unless sharpened to a chisel point! The pencil is only used for marking the timber, e.g. for face side, edge marks and chamfers. It should never be used to mark a line for sawing to: a knife is employed for this purpose, but must only be used across the grain in conjunction with a try square. I find that a small engineer's square is ideal for the small pieces of wood necessary for box making, and a larger woodworker's square is also useful for larger sections of timber.

Marking gauges are used with the grain. They can be difficult to use initially, but practice makes perfect. As they have a pointed spur to mark the wood, it will tear the grain if used across it. A **cutting gauge** is needed for this purpose, as the spur is replaced with a knife. When marking out dovetails, a very fine **scriber** is ideal.

Measuring is done mainly with a **steel rule**; a 150mm and 300mm rule provide all that is needed. A flexible steel rule is ideal for rough measurement.

CRAMPS

The first fact about cramping relates to Murphy's Law and states that 'You never have enough cramps!' Nowadays there is a tremendous variety of cramps available and I use G-cramps, quick action-style, sash, spring, elastic, frame, web, the superb Speed Frame and a variety of other cramps, some of which are home-made for particular purposes (*see* Fig 2.5).

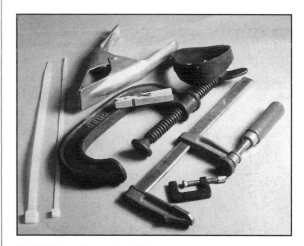

Fig 2.5 Various cramps: G- and F-cramps, spring cramp, plastic ties, inner tube and clothespeg.

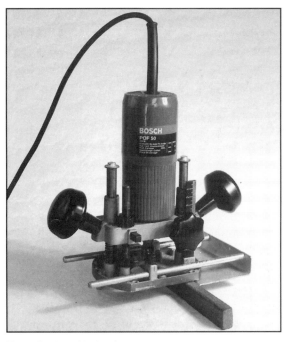

Fig 2.6 Small portable electric router.

Some tools referred to in the projects are by no means essential, but do make life a great deal easier. However, they tend to be expensive, and therefore I would not recommend buying them unless you can justify the expense. Of these tools, the portable **electric router** is the best known and probably the most useful (*see* Fig 2.6). It is a relatively new invention, and is proving a most useful piece of equipment. I use a small Bosch router, and this copes very well with the type of work needed in box making (*see* Chapter 5).

The other luxury tool is a **mitre saw** (*see* Fig 2.7). This is a device that uses a frame saw in a jig arrangement, which enables boxes of 4, 5, 6 or 8 sides to be cut repeatedly with great accuracy. As with routers, prices vary a great deal, and you obviously get what you pay for.

Fig 2.7 Mitre saw.

3

JOINTS AND TECHNIQUES

It is very rarely essential to use a particular joint for a box. Because most boxes do not require great strength in use, joints can be selected for ease of construction or for a decorative purpose. Some boxes are very definitely utilitarian in use, and do not need great care in constructing difficult and complex joints.

There is a feeling among some people that 'frank' joints, which display themselves, are preferable to those where everything is hidden. Dovetail joints are placed in this latter category: some say, 'Why spend a great deal of time in jointing mitred secret dovetails, when nobody can see anything other than a straight mitre joint?' Many craftsmen, however, feel that making a mitred secret dovetail joint is the highest form of woodworking, and its construction brings tremendous satisfaction and personal pride.

Whichever joint is decided upon, construct it to the best of your ability. Do not allow yourself to remain in a rut by only using one type of joint, but experiment and practise to improve your range of joints and your quality of work.

A good idea is to set your own personal standard and learn to accept nothing of a lower standard. Many years ago I decided that all my work would be stamped with my initials, provided that it reached the standard that I had set. Any lower standard was totally unacceptable. I still follow this practice, because it gives a target at which to aim. I am not prepared to accept a low standard, and neither should any self-respecting craftsman!

One final point: glues are not intended as gap fillers – in fact, some are useless in this respect, as they break down if the glue line is too thick. Aim always for snug fits, because there is nothing worse than a thick glue line, especially on small objects like boxes.

Before we look at the various joints in detail, it is worth mentioning the procedure for the assembly of boxes. Much of the following is also applicable to other forms of woodwork, but when applied to boxes it is worth remembering that small errors can look exaggerated.

Always prepare your work with care. It might sound old-fashioned to prepare the timber by planing each piece of material in sequence, but it does save a great deal of trouble in the long run.

Begin by planing the 'face side' by laying the timber flat on the bench top against the bench stop. The face side should always be the best, and it is planed dead flat and straight without being in 'wind' when the timber is twisted along its length. Check the surface by using a good quality straightedge, such as a steel rule, both along its length and across its diagonals.

When it has been planed correctly, mark it as shown in Fig 3.1 with a letter 'f', so that the tail points to the 'face edge'. This is now planed in the vice. When planed accurately, it should be straight and at right angles to the face side. Mark with a 'v', pointing to the face side mark.

Mark the required width on the face and opposite side, using a marking gauge. It is essential that the stock of the gauge is in constant contact with the face edge. Make sure that the spur trails along the wood: do not have the spur so vertical that it tends to dig into the wood. If necessary, go over the line several times rather than trying to get a definite line in one.

Having marked the wood, plane down to the line. The fourth side is treated in the same way. As only the face side and edge are checked in any way, it is important to remember that all further marking out is done from these two sides only, and the try square and marking gauge should only be used from these two surfaces.

It is almost always preferable to clean up and polish all internal surfaces prior to final assembly, for three very good reasons. First, if this is attempted afterwards, it is almost impossible to glasspaper the insides, especially in the corners.

Second, it is much easier to polish when in the unassembled state, as you do not have to worry about getting into corners. Third, surplus glue wipes off polished surfaces easily. Glue does not hold on polish, so remember not to polish over any part of a joint.

When assembling rectangular carcases, it is important to make sure that the frame is square. It is not good enough to rely on a try square, and the only accurate test is to measure the diagonals (*see* Fig 3.2). Geometry states that a rectangular object must have opposite sides of the same length, that the corners meet at right angles and that the diagonals must be equal. When these conditions are met, the frame will be square. In practice, it is easy to check that the opposite sides are equal. The diagonals can be measured with a thin steel rule or with a diagonal measuring strip (*see* Fig 3.3).

Any slight difference in the diagonal measurement can be altered by angling the cramps to 'push' the frame one way or the other. This can be seen in Fig 3.4; the cramps should be moved in the direction shown by the arrows.

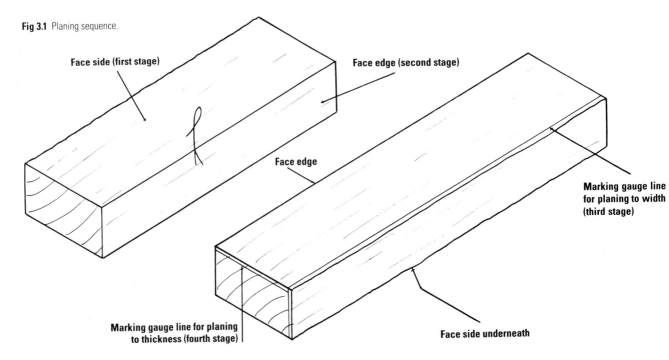

Fig 3.1 Planing sequence.

Face side (first stage)

Face edge (second stage)

Face edge

Marking gauge line for planing to width (third stage)

Marking gauge line for planing to thickness (fourth stage)

Face side underneath

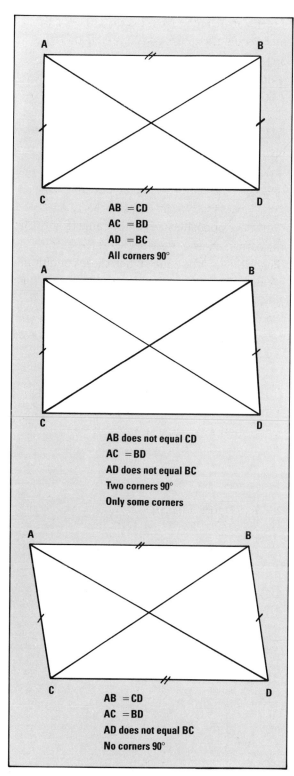

AB = CD
AC = BD
AD = BC
All corners 90°

AB does not equal CD
AC = BD
AD does not equal BC
Two corners 90°
Only some corners

AB = CD
AC = BD
AD does not equal BC
No corners 90°

Fig 3.2 Measuring the diagonals.

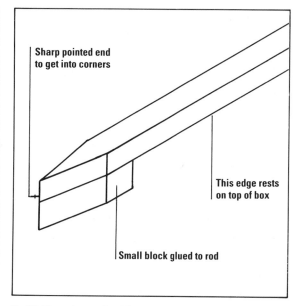

Sharp pointed end
to get into corners

This edge rests
on top of box

Small block glued to rod

Fig 3.3 Diagonal measuring strip.

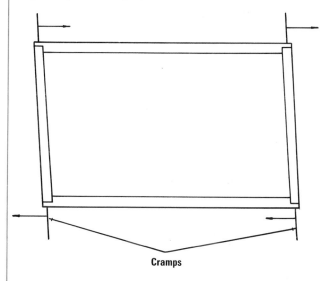

Cramps

Fig 3.4 Correcting out of square cramping.

When applying pressure with cramps such as G-cramps or sash cramps, protect the surface of the wood with scrap timber. Be careful not to apply too much pressure, as it is possible to bend the timber and also to squeeze out so much adhesive that the joint is starved of glue. Placing the cramps away from the joints will also cause the sides to bend inwards.

Fig 3.5 Mitre cutter and cramp.

It is always advisable to cramp initially without glue. This ensures that problems are spotted before glue sets, and also that cramps and protective blocks are collected together and made or set to the correct size.

BUTT JOINT

This is the simplest and humblest of all joints (*see* Fig 3.6), but it still requires care in order to be made to a satisfactory standard. This joint relies solely on a good fit and good quality glue. As glue is not very good on end grain, it is essential that care is taken.

This joint can be used at a corner or in the middle of a piece of wood. It is generally at right angles to the bottom and its adjoining piece, but not necessarily so. The work needed is similar for any required angle.

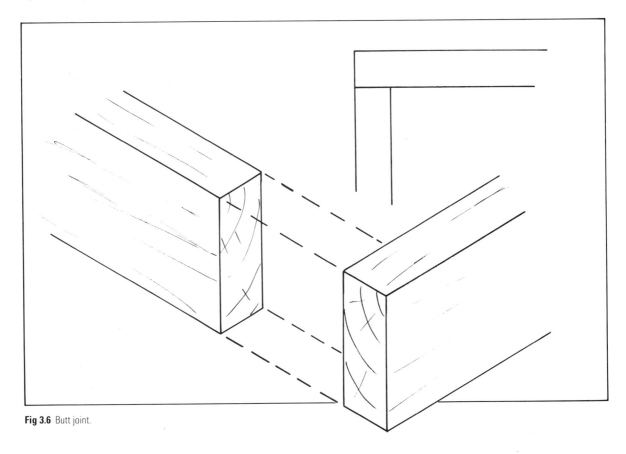

Fig 3.6 Butt joint.

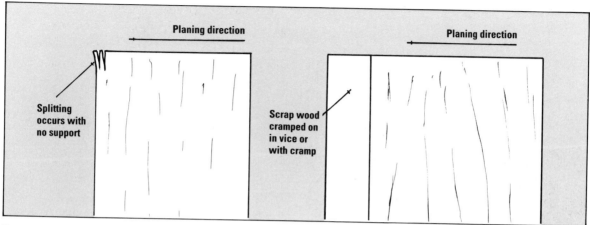

Fig 3.7 Planing end grain.

Mark off the correct length of each piece of wood with a square and knife, and then saw slightly on the waste side of the line. The ends now need to be planed flat and true to the chosen angle, usually at right angles. Hold the wood against a scrap piece of timber, preferably across the vice, and plane the end to the knife line, using a block or a smoothing plane (*see* Fig 3.7). The scrap piece supports the end grain of the timber and prevents the grain splitting. Be sure to plane towards the scrap timber so that it, rather than the required piece, will be ruined!

If you have never planed across end grain, it is worth doing so without a supporting piece of scrap. This will remind you forever of what is likely to happen! On larger width boards it is possible to plane without the supporting piece by planing from each edge towards the middle.

When planed, the ends can be coated with glue and cramped into position until the glue is dry. As this joint is more generally used for rough construction, nails or panel pins can be driven in to give added strength. The joint can also be strengthened by gluing blocks into the corners.

It is generally not possible to work a groove or rebate in a butt joint to take a panel for the bottom without a hole showing when the joint is assembled. One possibility is to stop the groove before it reaches the end of the piece, which will show the end grain when it is assembled. Alternatively, the small groove could be filled with a small piece of wood to close the groove. Neither of these remedies is really worth considering; if it is essential to have a groove or rebate, I would recommend the use of a different joint.

REBATED AND BUTT JOINT

This joint is considerably stronger than the butt joint because the gluing area is greatly increased; it also allows materials of different thicknesses to be used if necessary.

Using a knife and square, mark off the length of the two sides. Mark off the thickness of the wood on the inside faces and the edges, again using the knife and square. Set a marking gauge to between half and two-thirds of the thickness of the timber (*see* Fig 3.8), and mark across the end grain and the two edges down to the knife line.

Use a wide chisel to cut a V into the knife line, remembering to work from the waste side (*see* Fig 3.9). This provides a positive location for the saw and gives a cleaner shoulder line when cut.

Carefully saw down to the line and remove the waste with a chisel, working in from each end until the gauge line is reached. Take particular care to

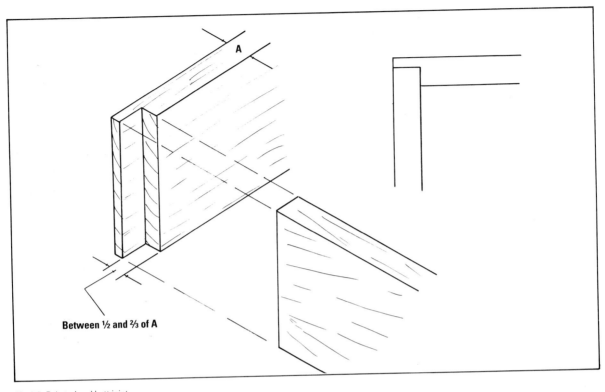

Fig 3.8 Rebated and butt joint.

see that the chiselled surface is as smooth as possible, and that it is flat.

The ends can now be prepared as for the butt joint and the box can be assembled when the joints have been checked.

Unlike the butt joint, it is common practice to work grooves or rebates to receive the bottom panel with this joint.

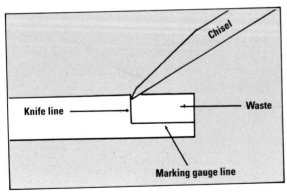

Fig 3.9 Chiselling a V groove on a knife line.

MITRE JOINT

Prepare your material accurately to size, especially to thickness, as this must be the same on each piece. The mitre joint is not as straightforward as it may appear: it is only a little stronger than the butt joint, and so a good fit is necessary. This is one joint where a device – the mitre saw – is very useful in cutting, but it is by no means essential.

Cutting by hand needs care, especially in the marking out stage. Use a mitre square set at 45°, or set a sliding bevel to this angle, using a set square as a guide. Mark this angle across the edge, and knife a line down the inside surface with the assistance of a try square. Mark the second edge at 45°, and finally knife the remaining surface. Either plane down to the line or remove most of the waste with a saw, and then plane.

It is essential to keep the plane flat on each part, so that the two mating surfaces meet properly. To

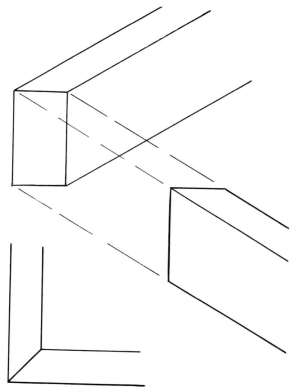

Fig 3.10 Mitre joint.

give a larger surface for the block plane, it is possible to plane two mitres together.

Using a proprietary device such as the Marples mitre cutter is easy, because the saw is held vertical and at the correct angle. A mitre saw is more sophisticated, in that it has its own frame saw, which can be set to many different angles (including 45°). Using either of these only requires that the opposite sides finish at the same length. The joint can be glued without further preparation – apart from perhaps the removal of a few whiskers (*see* Fig 3.10).

Mitre joints can be considerably strengthened by the addition of 'keys'. These are usually made from veneer on small boxes, but thicker material can be used. The grain direction in the keys must be along the length of the kerf, in order to utilize maximum strength. Their use can also be a decorative feature when the keys are cut from a

timber that contrasts in colour with the main box material. When the box is glued up, it can be marked out for the keys in one of two ways. Both ways are used in projects later in this book (*see* Chapters 12 and 17).

In the first instance, shown in Fig 17.1, the keys can be set in parallel to the top edge. The more traditional method sets them in a dovetail fashion. The frame needs to be marked out in the chosen manner and to a depth not more than two-thirds into the corner from the edge.

Holding the frame in a key-cutting cramp, a device described in Chapter 4, saw on the marks to the required depth. It is important that the saw chosen produces a kerf of the same width as the key's thickness. I use any one of four back saws, and have sometimes even resorted to a hacksaw with two blades fitted into its frame to produce the necessary width of cut.

The material chosen for the keys is then glued into each kerf. When set, each protruding part of the key is carefully removed with a chisel or plane, working in from the corner.

The other type of key is now used more widely than in the past. This employs a dovetail-shaped block of timber in a contrasting colour, which is glued into a corresponding slot (*see* Fig 3.12).

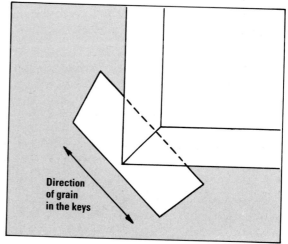

Direction of grain in the keys

Fig 3.11 Keyed mitre joint.

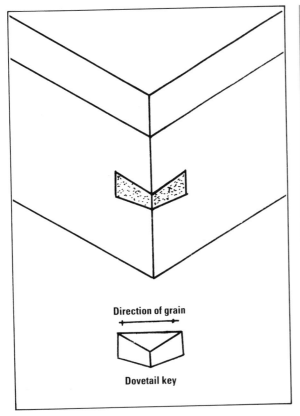

Direction of grain

Dovetail key

Fig 3.12 Solid dovetail keyed mitre joint.

When this type of key is used, it needs to be well shaped and reasonably fine, or it tends to look far too heavy and very ham-fisted. It can look especially good on triangular boxes. The side angle of the block needs to be 1:8, as for standard dovetail joints. It is much more difficult to cut than for veneer keys, and much care is needed in marking out and cutting.

DOVETAIL JOINTS

The dovetail joint is rightly described as the Rolls-Royce of woodworking joints. There is much mystique surrounding dovetails, so much so that many novice or inexperienced woodworkers shy away from even the consideration of using them! Much of this fear is not really sensible, as some of the types are relatively easy to execute with care.

However, it would be sensible to practise on some scrap timber before committing really good material to the fire.

There are several types of dovetail joint, but for boxes only the through or common dovetail and the secret mitre dovetail are generally needed.

As with the cutting of all joints, it is worth remembering that a saw removes a fine line of timber. Saw down the waste side of the line, so that the remaining timber is the size that is required. It is better in the long run not to chisel the sides of dovetails, but to leave them from the saw. In order to achieve this, you need to use a sharp, fine-cut saw.

A dovetail saw is made especially for such work, and should have at least 14 teeth per 25mm. The saw that I have come to favour for this type of work is a very fine back saw called an *ikedame*, made by the Japanese to a traditional pattern. This saw cuts on the pull rather than the push stroke, and is therefore unusual to European users. However, it is easy to adopt a new style like this, and I find that the benefits far outweigh the disadvantages. This saw produces a very fine kerf, and even enables a very fine shaving to be cut from end grain.

Tools required for dovetail cutting include:

- dovetail template or sliding bevel
- pencil
- marking knife
- cutting gauge or marking gauge
- dovetail saw
- scriber
- try square
- coping saw
- chisels

Much has been written on the way in which dovetails are to be set out, but very few descriptions are for anything other than straightforward joints, probably because decorative sequences are best left to the individual concerned.

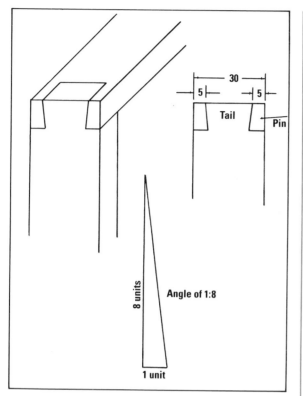

Fig 3.13 Marking out a dovetail.

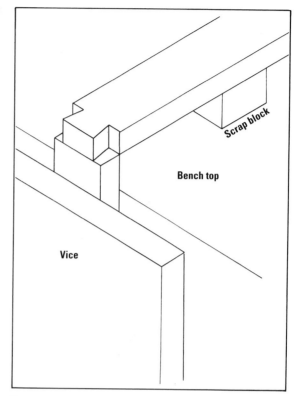

Fig 3.14 Aligning the wood.

The joint gets its name from the shape displayed by a dove's tail when the bird is landing. On either side of each 'tail' in the joint are the 'pins'. There will be several tails cut on most projects, sometimes of equal size and shape, although the arrangement is often altered to suit the need of a project or to provide a visually interesting pattern. The description which follows illustrates the cutting of a single-tailed joint and will be later developed into more complex versions.

Prepare a piece of timber to size, say for this exercise 200mm × 30mm × 12mm, making sure that the face edge and side marks are clear. (I appreciate that this is quite a large section, but it is a good size for the beginner to work with.) Square around at about the middle of the timber with a knife and square, and then cut accurately to the line with a tenon saw.

Set the cutting gauge to the thickness of the wood and mark from the cut ends on each piece. The piece for the tails needs to be so marked all round, but the pins only need to be marked across the width. On the end grain of the tails mark square to the sides, the size of the tail. For this exercise follow the measurements in Fig 3.13.

Mark in pencil down the tail using a dovetail template or a sliding bevel set to an angle of 1:8. (Do not use a knife for this, as the blade will follow the grain.) Place the wood in the vice at an angle so that the line that will be sawn is vertical.

Carefully cut with a dovetail saw to the line, stopping at the cutting gauge line. Do not cut deeper, as a cut will show up badly when the joint is finished. Turn the wood in order to cut the waste away, but again saw accurately to the line. At this stage you should have a tail cut, standing alone and clear.

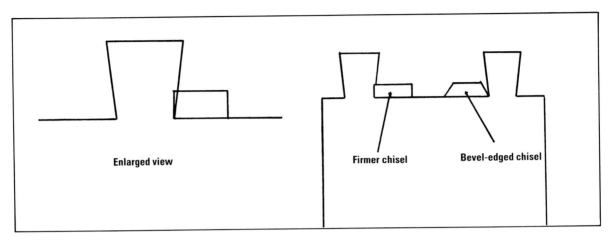

Fig 3.15 Using a bevel-edged chisel.

Hold the other piece of wood in the vice so that it stands proud of the surface to the height of a piece of scrap material (*see* Fig 3.14). Place the tail on the end grain, carefully align it, hold it down and mark the edge of the tail with a sharp and fine scriber, marking firmly so that the resulting marks are clear. Remember the old adage, 'measure twice and cut once', and check that the marks are correct and in the right place.

When you are satisfied that the marks are good, use a pencil and square to mark down the sides of the pins. Hold the wood vertically in the vice and saw down on the waste side of the lines to the gauge mark, aiming to saw so that the edge of the saw is just on the line; this way, little work will be needed later. Remove most of the waste with a coping saw, then place the wood on a chopping board on the bench and work back to the line with a chisel, taking care to finish on the line.

Provided you have worked accurately throughout the operations, the two pieces should now slide together to produce a tight fit. If there are gaps, start again, but if the joint is too tight, trim back the pins with a chisel until a fit is achieved. At this stage in a project, the timber would be cleaned up and assembled, the final stage being to plane the outside when the glue has set.

It is important that bevel-edged chisels are used when cutting dovetails, to prevent cutting into their sides (*see* Fig 3.15). Cutting wider boards with several tails follows exactly the same procedure,

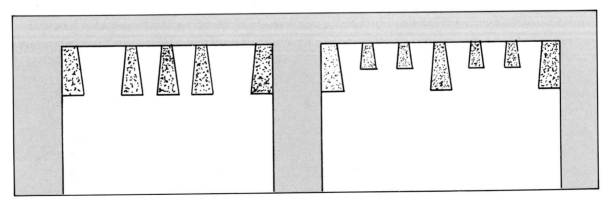

Fig 3.16 Dovetail patterns.

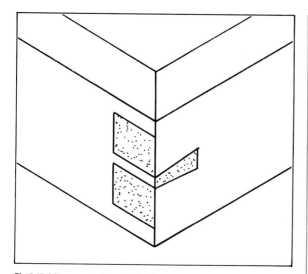

Fig 3.17 Mitres worked on outside edges.

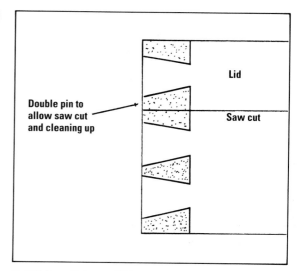

Fig 3.18 Dovetails for cut-off lids.

but there is obviously room for more mistakes, so it is essential that you work steadily and with a great deal of care.

Many projects employing dovetails can be made to look very good by cutting tails of different size and grouping them together in pairs. It is also possible to cut short tails as part of a sequence, as shown in Fig 3.16.

It is often desirable to construct these joints so that a rebate or groove for a top or bottom is hidden. This is achieved by mitring the outside pins. Should this be necessary, it is easy to cut with the saw down the full width of both parts instead of sawing just to 45° on the outside of the end tails (*see* Fig 3.17).

When using dovetails for a box that is to be cut to provide a lid, modifications are needed to accommodate the cut-off. To maintain strength, the cut must go through the centre of a pin, which needs to be wider to allow for the saw cut, as illustrated in Fig 3.18.

In boxes, the tails are usually placed on the front and back surfaces, but there are times when it is essential that they are cut on a particular surface, e.g. when making a briefcase: the tails must be on the vertical surface when the briefcase is being

carried, because their shape will 'lock' and therefore stop the weight of the contents pulling the joint apart. In this instance, there is likely to be no problem, even if the pins were to be worked on the verticals, as the weight is not too great. The matter, however, becomes very important when, say, a hanging bookcase is constructed, as fitting the wrong way round could eventually lead to all the books ending up on the floor when the joints pull apart!

MITRED SECRET DOVETAIL JOINT

Some people regard this as the most difficult joint in the vast array of jointing methods, and therefore the one to be avoided at all costs. It must be admitted that it is a difficult joint to make, but it is not really outside the scope of any who are prepared to take care in the various stages. Much of the work is difficult only because accuracy is important, and some stages are troublesome because a clear view is not always possible.

Both pieces must be exactly the same thickness and cut to the exact length needed. Begin by marking the thickness of the timber from each end (*see* line A in Fig 3.19). Now gauge the lap on each

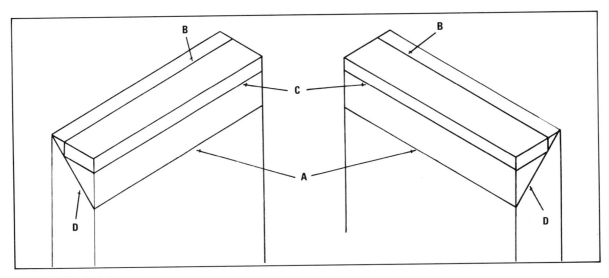

Fig 3.19 Marking the timber.

end (line B) and on the inside surfaces (line C). Mark the mitres on the outside edges using a marking knife and a mitre square (line D); this completes the initial marking out.

Referring to Fig 3.20, carefully cut the rebates with a dovetail saw, and then gauge the width of the lap on the edge mitres (line E). The pins should now be marked out on one of the ends – note that they are pins, and not the tails as described in the common dovetail. This is for ease, as it is almost impossible to cut the tails first and

then to mark the pins from them. It may be easier if a dovetail template is specially made to sit in the rebates; using an angle of 1:6 will also make life a great deal easier.

Cut the pins and then the edge mitres and finally in this stage, the mitres on the ends, as shown in Fig 3.21.

This is the critical stage, as mistakes will be almost impossible to remedy, so take a great deal of care and use sharp saws and chisels for this operation.

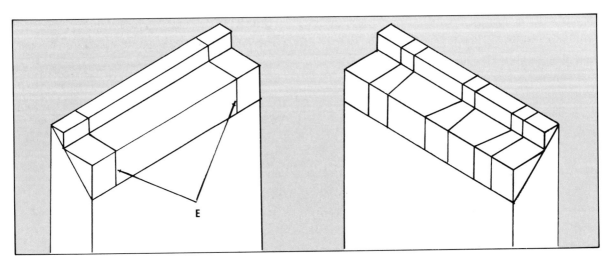

Fig 3.20 Marking the pins.

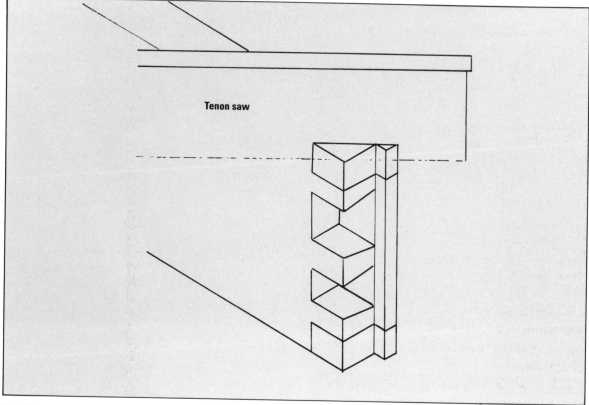

Fig 3.21 Cutting the mitres.

Finish the end mitre with the aid of a shoulder plane (*see* Fig 3.22), remembering to work from each end towards the middle to prevent the edges breaking out. It is also helpful to cramp a scrap piece of timber, also cut at 45°, to the outside surface to support the shoulder plane.

Mark out the tails from the pins using a fine and sharp scriber, square the lines over the top and double-check the marking. When satisfied, cut the tails and then the mitres as for the description on the pins. Dry-assemble and make minute adjustments as necessary.

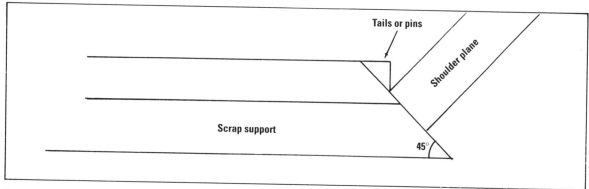

Fig 3.22 Finishing the end mitre.

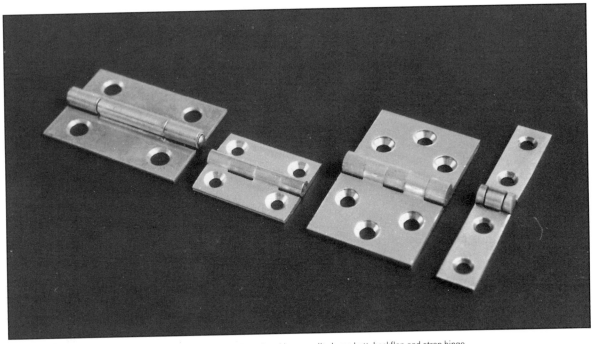

Fig 3.23 From left to right: cheap butt hinge, quality brass butt, backflap and strap hinge.

HINGING

The most commonly used hinge is the butt hinge, which is available in a variety of sizes and finishes. Most small boxes will need only 18mm or 25mm butts, preferably made from solid drawn brass (*see* Fig 3.23). Many brass hinges are now made from thin sheet brass pressed into the required shape, but these are not good quality and are best avoided for good quality work.

There are no hard and fast rules for determining the position of hinges, but I tend to set them about their own length from the inside corner of the box, as shown in Fig 3.24. If possible, cramp the lid to the back side of the box and mark the position of both hinges with a knife and square.

Set a marking gauge to the centre of the hinge pin to the open side, and transfer this distance to the box between the knife lines, to mark the width of the hinge (*see* Fig 3.25). Using the same tools, set the depth of half of the hinge and transfer this to the back sides of the lid and box (*see* Fig 3.26).

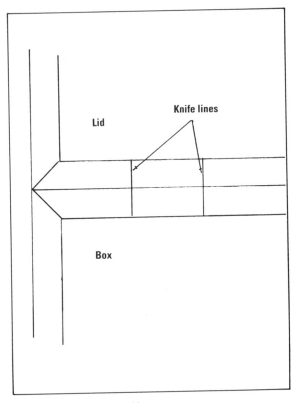

Fig 3.24 Marking the hinge positions.

26

Remove the waste with a saw and chisel, taking care not to break out the small section of wood on the inside of the box: a good idea is to cramp a piece of scrap on the inside to strengthen and protect while chiselling (*see* Fig 3.27).

Use only one screw to initially fix the hinges, in case a mistake has been made and needs to be remedied. When satisfied with the fit, drive the remaining screws into position.

Measurements must be accurate at all times to achieve a good fit; problems will arise if the housing is cut too deep and then needs to be packed with a piece of veneer to bring the hinge surface level with the surface. The countersinks for the screw heads are often too shallow, making the head of the screw proud: either use a smaller gauge of screw or increase the depth with a countersink bit. It is also important that the recess is flat; if not, the result is unsightly and also puts undue strain on the hinge.

Use steel screws to initially fit the hinges, and then replace them with brass screws of the same length, gauge and screw pattern. Brass screws have a penchant for breaking off far too easily, so techniques to prevent this happening are wise precautions.

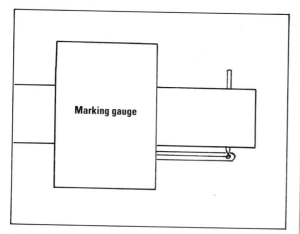

Fig 3.25 Setting the marking gauge for the width.

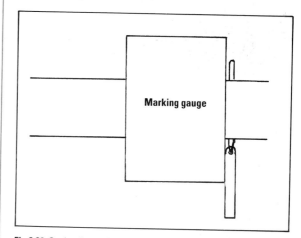

Fig 3.26 Setting the marking gauge for the depth.

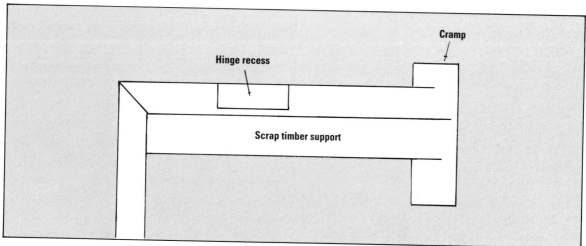

Fig 3.27 Using scrap while chiselling.

The other alternative to setting the hinge into both parts of the box is to set it entirely into one surface. I feel that this does not look as good, and often leads to inaccuracy in the lining up of the top and bottom.

LEATHER

I frequently use leather in the lining of boxes: it has a rich appearance and adds a certain quality to the work. It is best cut on a flat board, held into place by a heavy rule (preferably of a safety pattern) and cut with a sharp knife. Over the years I have favoured the use of knives of the Stanley type: blades are readily available, and a sharp one should always be to hand.

As far as fixing is concerned, there is a choice of at least two adhesives. I mostly use Copydex, but any of the contact adhesives, such as Thixofix or Evo-stik, are equally suitable. Make sure that whatever adhesive is used, you follow the maker's instructions to the letter!

SMALL PIECE PLYWOOD CONSTRUCTION

There will frequently be a need to use small pieces of plywood for the lids and bases of boxes. It is possible, although difficult, to buy ply in very thin sections, i.e. under 2.5mm, but this is never produced with decorative facings. This leaves two alternatives of action: veneer a thin piece of ply or produce your own.

Plywood is made from thin sheets, or plies, of solid timber, glued together so that each sheet has its grain running at right angles to its neighbour. For stability, all plywoods are made with an odd number of layers or plies.

Cut the veneer to the required size, allowing extra for accurate trimming to size later. Remember that the alternate plies must have their grain running at 90° to the neighbouring ones.

Spread a thin coating of glue over one surface, place the next veneer in place, and then repeat the process until all plies are in place.

Wrap the ply in paper and cramp up between two thick pieces of MDF or chipboard until the glue has cured. I am fortunate in owning an old bookbinder's small cramping press that is ideal as it gives even pressure over the entire surface.

A word of warning: do not use too much glue, as the veneer will soak it up and take a long time to dry. Remember that wood is hydroscopic, and will therefore absorb a great deal of moisture.

When using commercial plywood, the surface will probably need to be veneered with your own choice of veneer. This can be glued on as already described above, or it can be glued using glue film. This is a hot-melt glue that is supplied in sheets and fixed to a release paper. An electric domestic iron will need to be warmed to a medium temperature for this procedure. Cut the film to size and choose one of the following methods of operation; try both, and continue to use the one that you prefer.

1 Iron the glue film on to the plywood and then release the paper. Locate the veneer, cover with the release paper to protect it from scorching, and iron until the glue sets. It will need heat all over the surface for 8–10 seconds.
2 Carefully remove the release paper, position the film and the veneer together and then apply the heat. This method requires only one application.

Producing your own plywood does use a lot of veneer, but has some advantages, particularly that the resulting ply can have the same colour throughout when needed. When this is unimportant, do as I do and use plain, cheap veneer for the inside laminates. With careful selection of veneer for the outside layers, it is possible to achieve stunning results of colour and natural pattern.

4

USEFUL GADGETS

Most trades and crafts have their own unique and specialised devices that make work much easier. Often the gadgets are not available commercially, but are handmade by the craftsman. We are told that 'necessity is the mother of invention', and this is certainly true in the woodworking shop: the master craftsman passed on his secrets to his apprentice, but only when it was necessary so to do!

Some of these gadgets are well-known, e.g. the bench hook, while others, e.g. the jig for holding boxes firmly to cut keys, are less so. Inevitably, times and circumstances conspire to show that a particular object is needed in a project, and it is then that a new idea comes to fruition.

The six gadgets described here are by no means all that could have been included, but they have all proved to be extremely useful.

Fig 4.1 Some of the author's well-used bench hooks.

BENCH HOOK

A selection of bench hooks of different sizes will prove invaluable. Basic designs are available commercially, but those as illustrated in Figs 4.1 and 4.2 are easy and cheap to make. The use of bench hooks allows wood to be gripped safely when sawing; they also protect the bench surface from damage. Left-handed people should construct the hook with the sawing gap on the left side of the board, while for right-handed people, the gap should obviously be on the right.

Select a piece of hardwood for the board and a strip for the two clamping sections – these must not be so large as to make them uncomfortable to grip. The section that holds to the edge of the bench or may be gripped in the bench vice should be the full width of the board; this gives stability when in use. I have found it helpful to groove the board on the intended sawing line with a width of about 10mm. Spot-glue a hardwood strip into the groove to hold it in position. When this has been cut beyond all recognition, it can be easily removed and replaced with a new piece.

Join the clamps to the board using dowels and glue. Sizes for bench hooks are very individual, but I make them from as small as 100mm × 70mm up to 450mm × 300mm. Although I have suggested the use of hardwoods here, I have also successfully used plywood, chipboard and MDF.

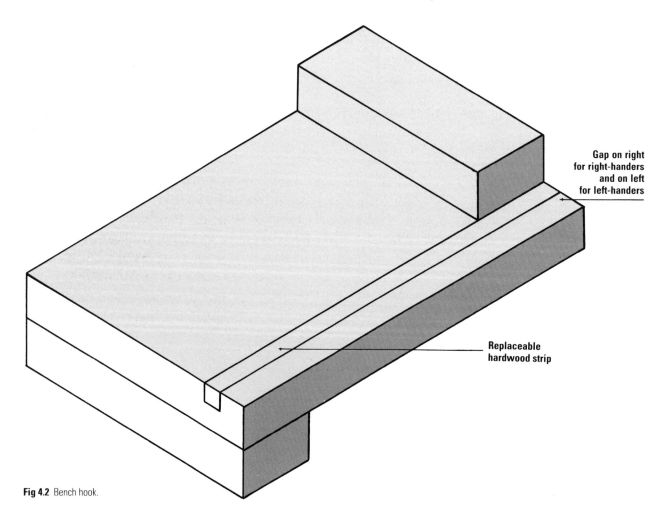

Gap on right for right-handers and on left for left-handers

Replaceable hardwood strip

Fig 4.2 Bench hook.

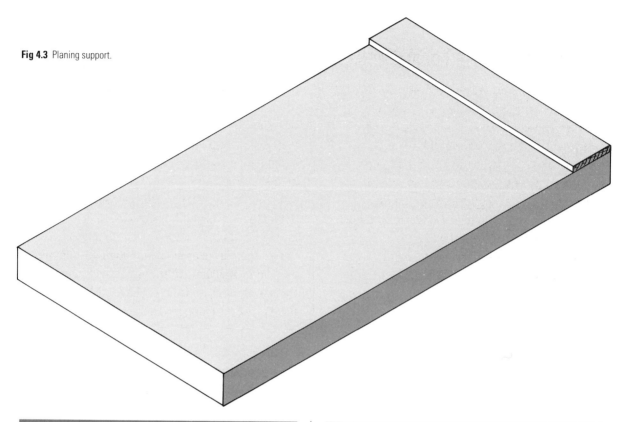

Fig 4.3 Planing support.

PLANING SUPPORT

Very thin sections of timber are difficult to control at the best of times, but trying to plane them on the bench top, or worse still in a vice, is almost impossible. A simple board of MDF with a lolly stick glued across it at righ angles, as shown in Fig 4.3, makes life so much easier! MDF is very stable, and so is ideal for the base board. The stop strip must be made from a dense hardwood to withstand the punishment it will receive. With modifications, as shown in the planing jig (*see* page 33), it could also be used to plane small pieces to thickness. A variety of sizes is again useful for this type of device.

V SUPPORT

Back in the 1950s I spent hours using one of these as a support for thin plywood when using a fretsaw. It merely consists of a rectangular board about 150mm × 100mm with a clamping strip fixed to it (*see* Fig 4.4). The strip can be housed in, dowelled on or just glued on as a butt joint. The V cutout is best kept as small as possible in order to provide as much support for the timber being worked.

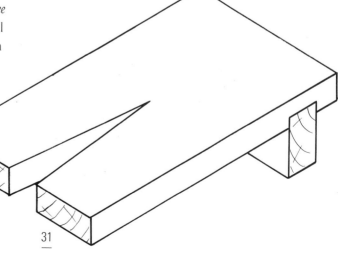

Fig 4.4 V support.

DOVETAIL TEMPLATE

Dovetail joints are made to have different slopes, depending on the type of wood being worked (*see* Fig 4.5). Over the years an angle of 1:8 has been accepted for hardwoods, and 1:6 for softwoods. A considerable amount of money was spent on research back in the 1950s to find the correct angle; I heard many an old craftsman muttering that it was a waste of money, because they could tell the scientists the correct angles. They were proved to be right!

These templates have varied a great deal in design, from the basic to the complex, but all do the same job in the end. (Some have even been given away as a present with magazines.)

Fig 4.6 illustrates a basic template that I have used for many years. Again it is worthwhile making a selection with different dimensions, but do use a hardwood. Those skilled in working metal will come up with ideas that are as easy to make as wooden templates.

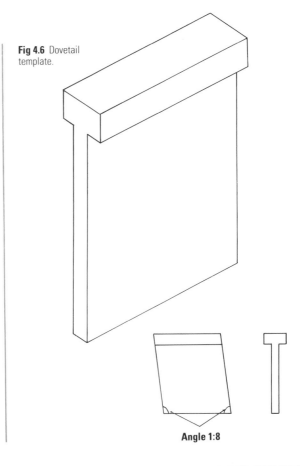

Fig 4.6 Dovetail template.

Angle 1:8

Fig 4.5 Handmade dovetail templates.

Fig 4.7 Key-cutting cramp.

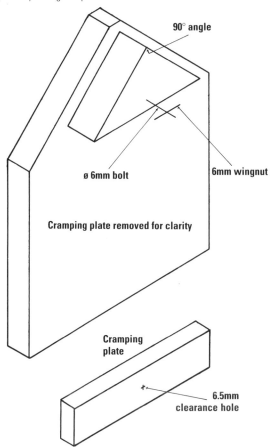

90° angle

ø 6mm bolt

6mm wingnut

Cramping plate removed for clarity

Cramping plate

6.5mm clearance hole

KEY-CUTTING CRAMPS

Keys are generally cut across the ends of mitre joints using a saw. End grain does not take glue very well; on a mitre joint, the holding properties will be somewhat better because the joint is not totally end grain. However, it is still very easy for a glued mitre joint to break down when further work is attempted. A simple jig will allow sawing keys to take place with no worries (*see* Fig 4.7).

A triangular block of material, such as chipboard or MDF, is glued to a backing board. It is a good idea to provide for several eventualities by having extra thicknesses that can be added should a larger depth of box be needed. These extra pieces can be dowelled on without using glue.

Drill a hole through both pieces to suit a bolt: a 6mm bolt with a wingnut is ideal. The box frame is cramped in place by a loose cramping plate, which is pulled down on the box by the wingnut (*see* Fig 4.8). This arrangement works well, and means that even a very thin-sided box can be held without any fear of the joint failing.

PLANING JIG

A jig of this nature is only worth making if a number of identical pieces are needed. By its very nature, it has to be made very accurately, or else all sections planed will also be inaccurate. Preparations must be thorough, with accurate marking out and planing.

Use only hard and stable material: MDF is ideal for the base board, but a good quality hardwood is really needed for the plane guides. Prepare these as shown in Fig 4.9, so that the rebate is about 10mm deep. The width of the rebate should be the same size as the solid bit of metal to the side of the plane mouth. This surface can be further improved by fixing a hard plastic strip on which the plane can run.

Fig 4.8 Key-cutting cramp.

Fig 4.9 Planing jig.

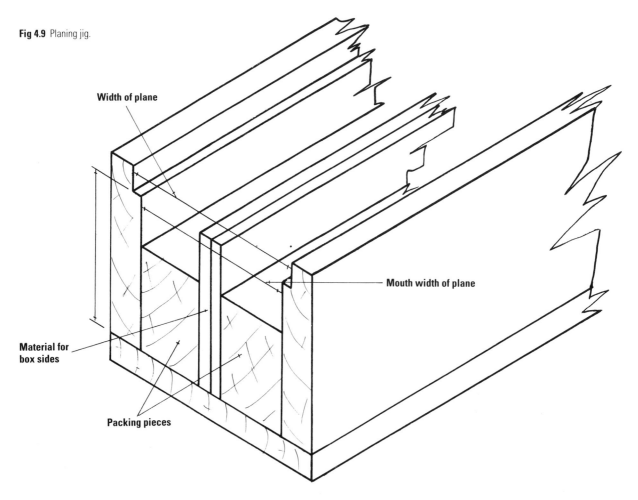

Width of plane

Mouth width of plane

Material for
box sides

Packing pieces

The depth between the bottom of the rebate and the top of the base board must be the exact size needed for the box strips. Fix these two pieces to the base board with screws and glue, taking care that they are fixed parallel to each other and the correct distance apart. The two packing pieces support the strips while they are being planed (*see* Fig 4.10). This jig will permit the planing of several strips at the same time, by just varying the widths of the packing pieces.

The same jig can be used for different width strips by adding plywood strips to the inside of the base board, to reduce the width that it is possible to plane. A stop needs to be fixed at one end to prevent the timber being pushed out by the action of the plane.

Fig 4.10 Planing jig in use.

5

VENEER BOXES

eneer has generally been used as a decorative cover on an inferior base. As mentioned in Chapter 1, it was originally sawn and therefore quite thick, but can now be produced as thin as 0.05mm. A large quantity of veneer is produced for the furniture trade from a vast variety of timbers, some quite plain and others very ornate. In this age where conservation is so important, this is one way of ensuring that a little goes a long way.

The idea of using veneer in boxes is by no means new. There are numerous examples of beautiful tea caddies which were often ornately veneered with many different and decorative timbers. However, using veneer only in construction is, I believe, quite unusual. Those made in this way are very light, and present new problems that need to be overcome, as well as providing tremendous satisfaction in their

Fig 5.1 Veneer moulds.

construction. Personal imagination and craft standard determine the outcome in this type of work; there is little room for mistakes and poor standards of work.

Most of the designs for these boxes rely on the construction of moulds in which the veneer is held while the glue sets. Get the mould wrong, and the finished box will reflect all its inaccuracies. It really does pay to spend a great deal of time and care on the preparation and construction of moulds. However, be prepared, as this time can take as long as, or even longer than, the construction of the box.

Modern science has provided us with a new material which is splendid for the construction of moulds; medium density fibreboard, or MDF as it is known. I have also used solid timber, chipboard and sundry other materials when the need has arisen. The portable electric router is a boon in this work, but very good results can be achieved by using hand tools.

Whichever method you use, care is the order of the day. There are two main types of mould: a one-piece mould, where the veneer is held against it, and a two or more-piece mould, which is used to cramp the veneer into shape. Both types generally require the surfaces to be flat and square to achieve a good fit of finished parts (*see* Fig 5.1) – it is so easy to produce a mould that is twisted and not accurate enough for these purposes.

The best way is to build up a mould to the required thickness with several layers of thinner MDF, 12mm or 18mm being ideal. This is not as easy as it sounds, especially when using only hand tools. With an electric router, it is best to use a template from a piece of plywood or similar material which is temporarily fixed to the MDF, the router then being guided around the template using the guide bush (*see* page 37). The layers are then glued together, making sure that each lines up exactly with its neighbours. Any slight discrepancy must be remedied when the glue has set.

When veneer is held between two parts of a mould, it is important that the gap between the parts equals the total thickness of the veneer plus a small allowance for paper or other protective material. Try to use a router cutter to match this measurement, as this saves a great deal of work and is also very accurate.

Before the mould is finished, sand its surfaces and polish thoroughly, to protect them and to ensure that any surplus glue can easily be removed later. In use, always place a few layers of paper wider than the veneer between the veneer and the mould; this helps to keep glue away from the mould and to cushion the veneer when the mould is cramped.

It is sometimes necessary to make a mould of more than two parts, e.g. when the shape of the laminate is complex and would be impossible to assemble and cramp if only two parts were used. Experience will soon show when this is necessary; the project in Chapter 28 employs this type of mould.

A wide range of cramps is employed in this work; in addition to sash cramps, a good range and number of G-cramps are very useful. A visit to the local car tyre centre for old inner tubes will prove worthwhile, as one of these will provide good elastic bands which make superb cramps. Web cramps are also a useful addition to the workshop equipment.

MAKING AND USING TEMPLATES FOR ROUTERS

As stated above, portable electric routers make life very much easier when making moulds for these veneer boxes: final accuracy is high, although very dependent on the initial preparatory work.

It is important that the mould is longer than required, so that waste is retained to allow for ease of working. The template material needs to be at least 8mm in thickness and of a hard and close-

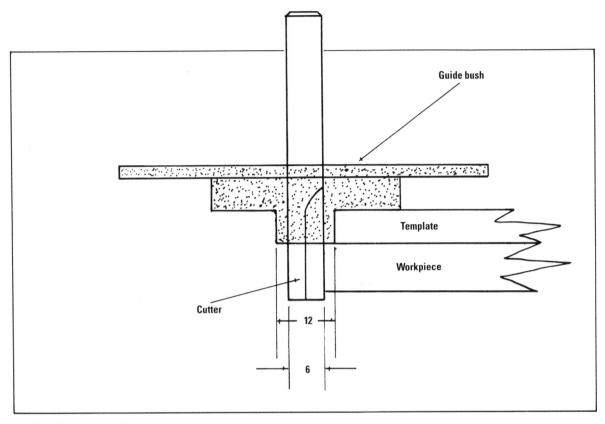

Fig 5.2 Guide bush and template system.

grained material. Good quality plywood, MDF or acrylic sheet are ideal, but as you will only be using the template a few times, it is not worth going to great expense.

I use an old, but reliable, Bosch POF50 router, and will therefore quote measurements for this machine; for others, consult the manufacturer's handbook. Internal and external cutting need different calculations to be made in order to arrive at the correct final measurements.

INTERNAL CUTTING

The template for internal cutting should be larger than the final measurements. Calculate the oversize by subtracting the cutter diameter from the bush outside diameter, and then divide by two. As an example, take a cutter of 6mm diameter. With a guide bush diameter of 12mm, the template would need to be 3mm larger all round than the required final measurement, as shown in Fig 5.2.

EXTERNAL CUTTING

Using the same size details as in the previous paragraph, the template needs to be 3mm smaller than the required size to achieve the desired result.

TEMPLATES IN USE

In use, the template should be fixed to the material that is to be cut. Several methods can be employed: the easiest is probably to tack the template into place with small panel pins. Cramping is also possible in some situations, but a wide, good quality, double-sided tape gives superb results.

With the guide bush fitted to the router base and the template fixed to the material, guide the router round the template, making several passes until the cutter pierces the material. The process is then repeated until you have sufficient pieces to make up the necessary mould thickness.

PROJECTS

*'To unite elegance and utility, and blend useful
with agreeable, has ever been considered a difficult,
but an honourable task.'*

HEPPLEWHITE

6

GLASSPAPER CONTAINER

One thing in my workshop that annoys me more than most is sheets of abrasive paper that have curled up into a roll! When the ambient temperature increases, so the paper takes on a life of its own. In winter, the opposite problem exists, and the paper absorbs moisture and is limp and useless. Paper that is not flat is more difficult to control and to cut properly into six pieces for use with a cork-faced block, as shown in Chapter 1.

It is a simple matter to make a container that will keep the paper flat, but it should still be presentable and not cobbled together in any manner with rough-looking timber.

A standard sheet of glasspaper is approximately 280mm × 230mm, but is still made to the imperial measurements of 11in × 9in. This means that the inside measurements need to be a little bigger than these in order to allow fingers to get around the side; about 10mm extra all round will do.

No strength is required for the corner joints, so a butt joint is fine, as long as you are accurate in cutting to length. The depth is made to 50mm (*see* Fig 6.1), but any size can be made to suit individual requirements.

METHOD

Select and prepare two end pieces 240mm long and the front and back to 304mm, assuming that you are using 12mm thick material. Mark accurately to length using a try square and knife, and cut slightly overlength.

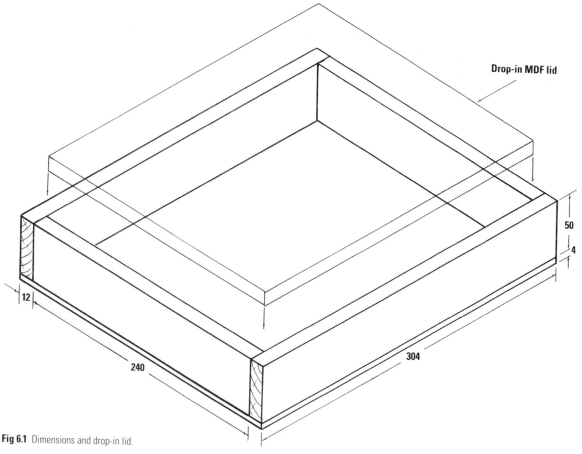

Drop-in MDF lid

50

4

12

240

304

Fig 6.1 Dimensions and drop-in lid.

The two ends must be exactly the same, and can be planed in the vice with a block plane. Use a piece of scrap wood at the far end of the pieces to make sure that the end grain does not split out. A useful tip is to hold the two pieces together with a couple of small pieces of double-sided tape, thus ensuring that they are more easily planed to the same length. Smooth the inside surfaces with a

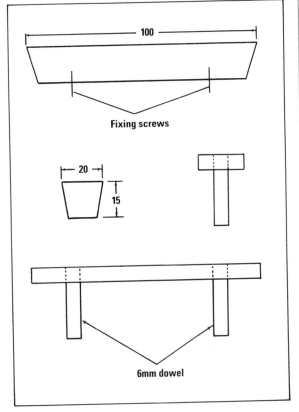

Fig 6.2 Handles.

smoothing plane and glasspaper, and cramp up dry to check that everything is in order.

Glue the pieces together and cramp up in sash cramps until the glue is set, remembering to check that the frame is square by measuring the diagonals. As glue does not hold very well on end grain, leave the frame in the cramps and plane flat the edges on show. Leaving the frame in the cramps gives more security and therefore less chance of breaking a joint apart.

Cut a piece of 4mm ply to slightly oversize, glasspaper one surface smooth and glue this surface on to the planed edge. To do this and to minimize the number of G-cramps needed, remove the frame from the sash cramps and place the plywood on a thick piece of chipboard, with the frame on top. Some protection to the top edge will be needed, in the form of pieces of timber, but this method only uses four G-cramps.

Leave cramped up until the glue has hardened, and then plane the outside surfaces smooth, glasspaper and then polish with oil or a hard plastic coating. A drop-in 'weight' is needed to apply pressure to the sheets to keep them flat, and a piece of chipboard or – preferably – MDF is cut to just drop in with very little clearance. This method works well, whether you have one or 21 sheets of paper to keep flat. A handle will be needed to lift this lid out, so design and make one to suit your own purpose – a couple of simple suggested designs are shown in Fig 6.2. This lid also needs to be protected with the finish used on the base.

SUGGESTED CUTTING LIST					
Lengths are gross, widths and thicknesses are net. All measurements in millimetres					
PART	NO. REQUIRED	LENGTH	WIDTH	THICK	MATERIAL
Sides	2	320	50	12	Softwood
Ends	2	250	50	12	Softwood
Base	1	320	250	4	Plywood
Top	1	290	245	12	MDF
Handle	1	100	15	15	Hardwood

7

TELEPHONE
NOTEBLOCK
HOLDER

I suspect that many of you, like me, can never find a piece of paper when you are speaking on the telephone. Having bought a noteblock from the local stationer, I then decided to make a holder for it.

After making several of these, and having bought different blocks of paper, I have realised that the blocks are not made to the same size. Most are approximately 90mm square, whilst some are 95mm × 90mm and others are nearer 100mm square. As a result, I make these holders to accommodate the largest size.

Almost any timber is suitable for this project; a bonus, as only small pieces are needed, together with a small piece of plywood or veneer.

This holder is a small, open box as can be seen from Fig 7.1, and so a variety of joints can be used,

although dovetails are not needed, as little strength is necessary, I use mitre joints, but even lap joints are suitable.

METHOD

Prepare the wood to strip form of 30mm × 7mm and then cut accurately to a length of 114mm, assuming that you intend to mitre the corners. Before cutting to length, if you have prepared one long strip for the sides, it will pay to rebate the bottom edge for the plywood base before doing any other cutting. If you are intending to employ other joints, you might have to amend the sizes. You can also increase the width of the strips to accommodate a deeper block of paper. Over the years I have used a variety of aids to cut mitres, but

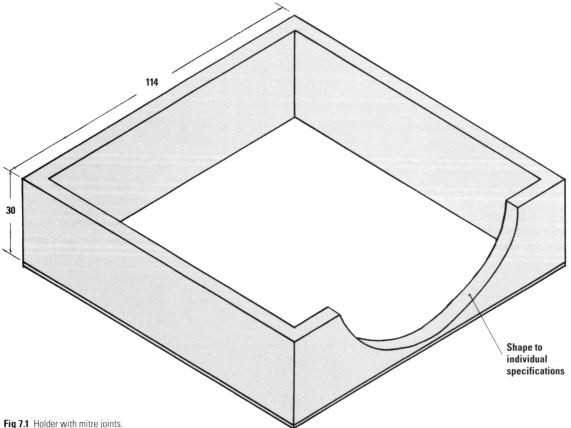

114

30

Shape to
individual
specifications

Fig 7.1 Holder with mitre joints.

the most convenient is either the Record mitre cutting cramp or the newer type of mitre saw, such as the Tyzack, which I find most suitable.

Cut the joints and check that you have a good fit, modifying as necessary. If you intend to use a rebated base and you did not rebate earlier, you must do so now. If the base is to be fixed only with glue, rebating is not really essential.

The cutout on the front is a free choice in shape, but I suggest a radius of about 40mm. Now clean up and polish the inside surfaces.

Gluing up small boxes can be a problem, but mitre cramps, frame cramps or web cramps are all suitable devices. I now use the Veritas Speed frame cramp, and find this a superb piece of equipment.

While the glue is setting on the frame, you need to make the base if you are using veneer. I prefer this, as I can match the base to the sides of the box; it also keeps the box very light. Cut three pieces of veneer to about 118mm square and glue them together in the same way as you would glue plywood. Protect the outside layers with paper and then cramp them between two strong, flat boards until dry.

When the box frame is ready, plane the bottom dead flat to take the base. Clean up the base, and glue and cramp it to the box until dry. Trim the base edges back flush with the sides, planing in from the mitres to avoid splitting out in the grain. Sand and polish with your favourite 'brew'.

SUGGESTED CUTTING LIST					
Lengths are gross, widths and thicknesses are net. All measurements in millimetres					
PART	NO. REQUIRED	LENGTH	WIDTH	THICK	MATERIAL
Sides	4	125	30	8	Hardwood
Base	1	125	125	3	Plywood

8

MAGAZINE
SLIPCASE

Like most woodworkers, I tend to keep magazines, but all too often they tend to be left in heaps in corners of cupboards, waiting for the day when they will be sorted into some order! Most magazine publishers sell folders to contain a year's offerings, but it is more challenging to make your own customized slipcase.

The internal size of the case needs to be slightly larger than the magazine size, and can be made to accommodate as many magazines as you wish. The choice of size is ultimately up to you because the size of magazines differs widely.

METHOD

Select a suitable timber and plane it to size, preferably as one length and 12mm in thickness.

Work a rebate on the two outer edges to take 4mm plywood, and cut the thickness of the timber into half before you cut the piece into the three strips that are needed (*see* Fig 8.1). A lap joint is preferable, as the joint will be easier to cramp than, say, a mitre joint.

It is a good idea to make a finger grip on the vertical piece to facilitate easy removal from the shelf. Mark out the centres required and drill the top hole only to a diameter of 14mm and a depth of 4mm. Drill the lower hole of 22mm diameter right through the wood, taking care to prevent the wood breaking out when the drill breaks through.

Cramp the wood in the vice and drill through until the point just appears on the back side, reverse the wood in the vice and drill through to finally remove all of the waste. Mark in the tangent lines and carefully pare away the excess timber.

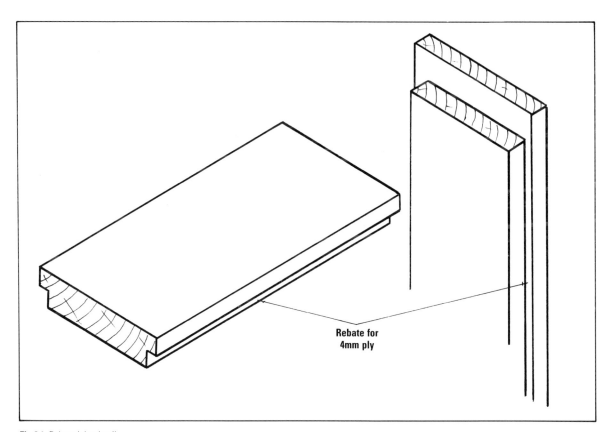

Rebate for 4mm ply

Fig 8.1 Rebate joint detail.

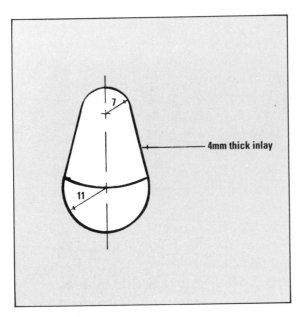

Fig 8.2 Finger grip.

Fig 8.3 The fingerpull in place.

Smooth up the inside of the bottom hole with glasspaper and then select a small piece of contrasting timber from your offcuts box; this will be fashioned into the finger grip (*see* Fig 8.2). Plane this piece a little thicker than is required, mark out the size and shape needed, and cut to fit the recess. Glue and cramp it in place, and when set, smooth the inside of all surfaces (*see* Fig 8.3). Using two sash cramps, glue the pieces together, taking care to check that the frame is square. Cut the plywood to be an accurate fit and glue it into the rebate.

Plane and glasspaper the outsides and finish with your chosen variety of polish. Finally, affix a label to the outside to identify your magazines.

SUGGESTED CUTTING LIST					
Lengths are gross, widths and thicknesses are net. All measurements in millimetres					
PART	NO. REQUIRED	LENGTH	WIDTH	THICK	MATERIAL
Front	1	335	50	12	Softwood
Top/bottom	2	245	50	12	Softwood
Pull handle	1	25	25	5	Hardwood
Sides	2	320	240	4	Plywood

9

PAPER TISSUE BOX COVER

here are several different makes of paper tissue on sale in the shops; many of the boxes are not very attractive to look at, so why not select some beautiful timber and cover up the cardboard box? It is important to research first in order to make the cover fit your chosen variety; the measurements supplied are one suggestion, but should be adapted as necessary. The cover needs to be very slightly larger than the cardboard box, so it is a good discipline to work accurately.

Very little strength is needed in the box, so any of the joints shown in this book can be used; the cover shown here is jointed with mitres.

METHOD

Select the timber and prepare it to the size needed. The two long sides should be grooved near the bottom edge to a width of 4mm, leaving about 4mm of solid wood on the bottom edge (*see* Fig 9.1); these grooves will support the strips which hold the box of tissues in place.

Cut the joints and check for a good fit before cleaning up the inside surface. Dry-cramping at this stage will ensure that you can glue up the frame accurately. When ready, apply glue and cramp up until set. While the cramps are still in place, plane the top edge level and smooth to take the top at a later stage and put the frame to one side.

The top needs to be prepared from a sound piece of wood to a slightly larger size than is needed. The hole in the centre of the lid should be the same size or slightly larger than the hole in the tissue box. If the hole is round, it can be marked easily with a pair of compasses; elliptical holes can be marked by using the push-out section from the box as a template.

Drill a small hole on the waste side of the line to take a coping saw blade, and saw around the line just on its inside. The wood is easily held on a V-shaped support which can be temporarily fixed to the bench in the vice.

Using a round-faced spokeshave, smooth the edge and round it off on both sides. Smooth it with

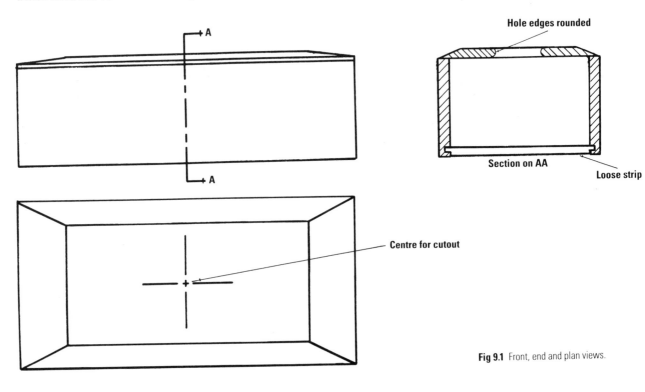

Fig 9.1 Front, end and plan views.

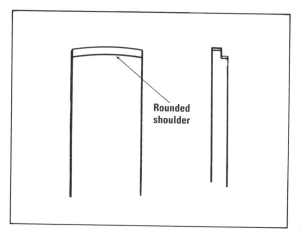

Fig 9.2 Support strip detail.

glasspaper and make sure that there are no rough edges which would catch the tissue when it is withdrawn (*see* Fig 9.1). Clean up the underside of the top, and glue and cramp it to the frame.

Plane the sides and chamfer or bevel the edges of the top before glasspapering and polishing.

Two strips 25mm wide × 7mm thick are now cut. The ends of each need to be rebated and the shoulders curved as shown in Fig 9.2. These strips should be a snug fit, but not so tight that force is needed to turn them in the grooves (*see* Fig 9.3). If a cube cover is made, use one strip only and make it 30mm wide.

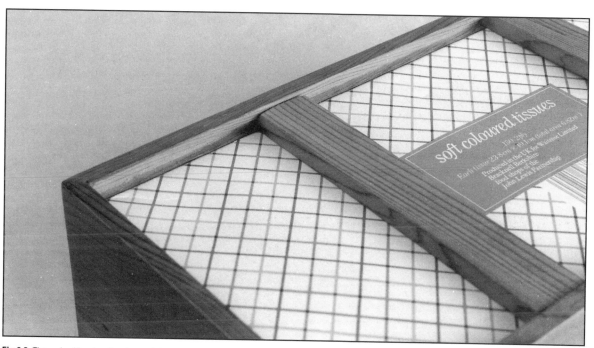

Fig 9.3 The underside, showing the retaining strips.

SUGGESTED CUTTING LIST					
Lengths are gross, widths and thicknesses are net. All measurements in millimetres					
PART	**NO. REQUIRED**	**LENGTH**	**WIDTH**	**THICK**	**MATERIAL**
Front/back	2	280	80	8	Hardwood
Ends	2	145	80	8	Hardwood
Top	1	280	140	8	Hardwood
Retainer clips	2	140	20	5	Hardwood

10

CARD BOX AND CRIB BOARD

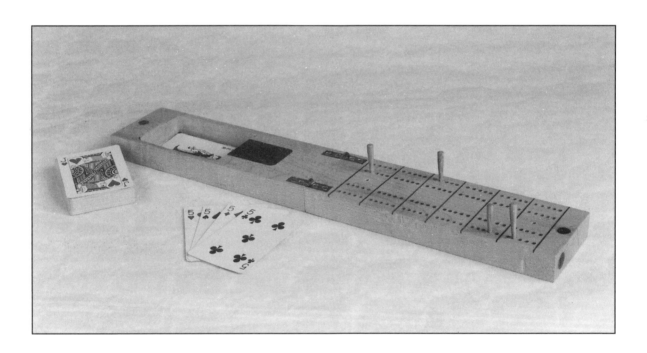

ribbage, or crib as it is more commonly known, is one of the oldest card games that is still played. Although in recent years it may not be as popular as formerly, it is still an excellent game to play. It is primarily a game for two, but three or four can play with little trouble.

The scoring depends on whether five, six or seven cards are dealt to each player; five cards are generally used, and the most usual score for winning is 61, hence the rows of 30 holes in the crib board, with one extra hole at the end of the board. Each side of the board has two rows of holes and is used by one player or team. (By the end of this project you will certainly have had plenty of experience of drilling holes in an accurate formation!) This enables each player to check that the opponent has scored correctly, and also provides a visual check on the relative state of each team.

The pegs are the markers, and are moved along the board to correspond with the number of points achieved at each scoring point. Life is made much easier when scoring if the holes are grouped together in rows of five; this also helps visually, as the board looks much better. It is, of course, possible to score with pencil and paper, but it is not as neat or convenient!

A block of hardwood to finish 380mm × 70mm × 20mm is needed for the main body, together with another of the same length and width but only 3mm thick. This second piece can be the same type or a contrasting timber.

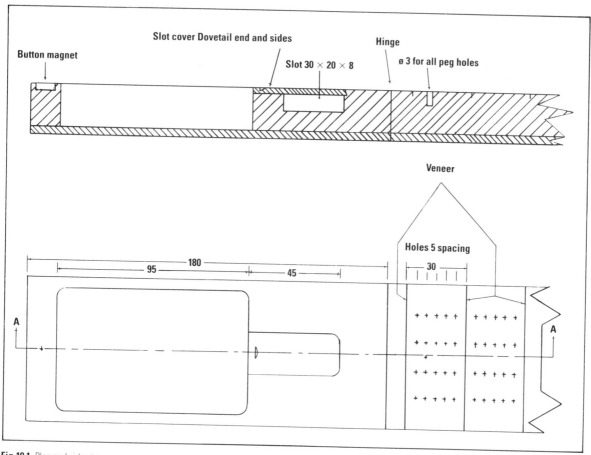

Fig 10.1 Plan and side views.

METHOD

Begin by planing the thicker piece of hardwood to size, and then mark off the length of each piece, allowing just over a saw kerf width between the two. Mark out the hole which will contain the cards to 95mm × 60mm, as shown in Fig 10.1. The corners need to be radiused to suit your drill size, but 8mm or 10mm would be ideal, so mark the centre for your chosen drill.

Cut the block in two and drill the corners. The edges of the card hole are now cut using a coping saw, and then finished by careful paring with a chisel followed by smoothing with glasspaper. (If using a portable electric router, the hole could be cut after a template has been made.) The small hole which will hold the pegs can be drilled or routed out to a depth of 9mm.

Cutting a dovetail side to the hole for the sliding lid is easy to work with a dovetail cutter in a router. The small lid for this slot needs to be a slightly tight sliding fit so that it only opens when needed. A small fingernail depression is carved into its top with a small gouge and chisel (see Fig 10.1).

The divisions between the sets of five holes on the other piece are made by sawing 2mm deep cuts spaced at 30mm, and then gluing in a piece of veneer. The holes are spaced as shown in Fig 10.1 and drilled to a depth of 6mm using a 3mm drill. Mark out the lines and the position for each hole.

Should you own a bench drill or a portable electric drill with a stand, fix a stop on the table so that the row of holes will end up in a dead straight line. Without such an aid, the drilling will need to be completed with care and good eyesight. Remember to drill the two extra holes between the centre rows at each end.

A more accurate way, although initially more time-consuming, is to make a drilling jig (see Fig 10.2). This can be simple or very involved, but it must be accurate because the final product will reflect all!

Fig 10.2 Hole drilling jig and centre bits.

The easiest construction is probably to use a small piece of angle, either ready-made or constructed by fixing two pieces together: cut this to the length of the distance between two veneer lines, making sure that the cut edges are finished smooth. The original was made to guide the drill for one double row of holes. The position for the holes can be marked out using squares, scribers, dividers, marking gauge or whatever is available.

There are two ways of doing the next step: when drilling into metal, especially with a small diameter drill, it is necessary to provide a 'start' for the drill in order to prevent it from skating about over the surface of the metal. For those with good eyesight, this can be done by placing a sharp centre punch on the metal in the correct position and striking with a hammer to create an imprint in the metal. This provides the necessary start for the drill, as the centre punch should be ground to the same angle as the point of a twist drill.

A second method, for the more skilful metalworker, is to mark each position with a centre drill; this will require the use of a good drill stand and vice. (Those with access to a vertical milling machine will have no difficulty in placing the holes accurately.)

When the jig is made, it is cramped in position on the crib board with a G-cramp, and used to guide the drill into the board to the correct depth.

Glue on the 3mm thick timber to the bottom of each piece, cleaning out any surplus glue inside the card slot before it sets.

Trim up the two hinged ends, taking care to make them straight and square. Good quality brass strap hinges are difficult to obtain in small sizes; a good alternative is to make them by cutting a back-flap hinge into two. You will have to file the cut edges smooth and straight, as well as possibly planishing the pin to stop the new hinge falling apart.

Fitting the hinges is exactly the same as fitting butt hinges (see Chapter 3). Take care with marking out and cutting so that the two sections line up properly when fitted. Any small discrepancy can be adjusted by planing the two pieces after the hinging is complete.

Remove the hinges and clean up and polish the completed board. A small catch is needed to keep the board closed up when it is not being used. Many varieties can be used, but probably the neatest and easiest to use is a small button magnet set into one side of the board, with a corresponding short length of steel set into the other half. This is done by drilling a hole of the correct diameter in the required position of each piece, preferably with a flat-bottomed drill. It is important that both the magnet and the matching

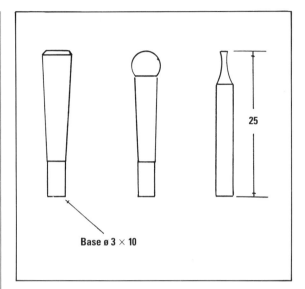

Fig 10.3 Peg shapes.

steel catchplate line up exactly, and that both are glued into position so that they are flush with the surface.

The pegs can be made from either wood or metal – Fig 10.3 shows three possible shapes. Rivets can be used, but silver rod would look much better; a small piece of silver rod is not very expensive, and is very easy to work with small hand tools. Note that silver rod is much firmer than wire of the same diameter, which will not really do a good job. Wooden pegs can be turned on a lathe as long as a good quality, straight-grained timber is used. They can even be made by hand if a great deal of care and patience are taken.

SUGGESTED CUTTING LIST					
Lengths are gross, widths and thicknesses are net. All measurements in millimetres					
PART	NO. REQUIRED	LENGTH	WIDTH	THICK	MATERIAL
Board and box	1	380	70	20	Hardwood
Top/bottom cover	1	380	70	3	Hardwood
Peg cover	1	45	22	3	Hardwood
Board dividers	7	75			Veneer
Pegs	4	25			Hardwood
Hinges	2 backflaps				Brass

11

SINGLE CARD BOX

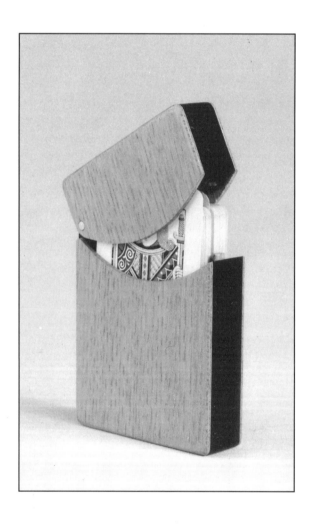

Playing cards are of ancient origin, and have long been popular items in households, both for playing and now as collector's items. In the fourteenth century their use was prohibited in Florence, while later in England, Queen Anne's government imposed a tax of sixpence on each pack, because gambling with cards was rife and this tax was hoped to be a deterrent!

The four suites of Hearts, Spades, Diamonds and Clubs are by no means universal, even in Europe, where different systems are used in the Germanic countries; some areas of the world even use circular cards. The packaging of packs of cards is not often good or attractive, and so a wooden case makes a great deal of sense. Although this box is small and employs the mitre joint, it is deceptively difficult to make; it is not a beginner's project unless great care is taken.

The front and back facings are made by gluing up a plywood of five layers of veneer. Select either veneers of the same type as the framework or those of a colour contrast; the box shown here was made from ebony and English oak, but for a really strong contrast try Indian rosewood and sycamore.

METHOD

Fig 11.1 shows front and side views of the box. The framework is prepared to a section of 18mm × 7mm by the respective lengths needed plus an allowance for waste.

The location pin will give you trouble at a later stage if you do not prepare for it now. Make sure that the ends are cut square and slightly overlength for the upright with the pin. Mark the centres for two 3mm holes on the end grain of the top of this piece. These need to be side by side so that their edges just touch on their insides.

If you have a bench drill, fix the piece upright and drill to a depth of at least 35mm. If using a hand drill, take care that the drill is kept exactly upright. Make sure that this piece is clearly marked to indicate that the end has been pre-drilled, otherwise when it is joined and glued up, you will have to guess.

Cut the mitres and test for accuracy, clean up the insides and then glue together. When the glue has set, carefully block plane the facing surfaces flat and true.

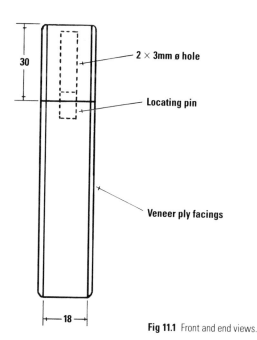

Fig 11.1 Front and end views.

Smooth the inside surfaces of the facing material. Hold the two surfaces together, insides touching, with a small piece of double-sided tape and mark the outside edges of the framework on to one piece. Mark out the curve, make marks for later lining-up purposes and cut to the line with the finest saw available. Smooth these edges by removing as little waste as possible. Separate the two plies and glue the bottom facings on to the framework.

When the glue has set, mark the position of the cut for the hinge pivot end and cut off square. This position is 10mm above the top of the facings at

Fig 11.2 The lid snapped shut.

this end. The front edge is cut to the line of the curve. The pivot end now needs to be rounded off on both pieces. Mark the semicircle and shape with a sharp chisel, and round off to the line before finishing with glasspaper. Take care, as this joint is not strong until the facings are fixed on both pieces.

The holes drilled earlier should now be carefully chiselled out to form a round-ended rectangle. If you do not have a small enough chisel for this purpose, try to make one out of a masonry nail. Should there be insufficient depth, drill out a little deeper. Shape a pin to fit tightly into the bottom hole to a depth of about 3mm and glue it in with about 5mm standing proud. The lid should be a snap fit on to the pin (*see* Fig 11.2).

When the glue has set, reassemble the box and glue on the top facings, taking care to line up the location marks. Plane the edges down to the frame, again using a block plane set finely. The pivot position is now marked and drilled to suit the pivot that you are going to use. Before fixing it, round off the bottom facing's back corner so that the lid can hinge clear without obstruction. Check for this before fixing the pin, which can now be glued in place. Glue only the head, using a cyanoacrylate adhesive (superglue).

Finally, clean up the entire outside and round off all exterior corners and edges. As this box will be handled a fair amount, make sure that the polish used will be suitable. Use Danish oil for a matt finish, and Clear Plastic coating for a gloss or semi-gloss finish.

SUGGESTED CUTTING LIST

Lengths are gross, widths and thicknesses are net. All measurements in millimetres

PART	NO. REQUIRED	LENGTH	WIDTH	THICK	MATERIAL
Sides	3	110	18	8	Hardwood
Top/bottom	2	80	18	8	Hardwood
Front/back	2 of 5 pieces	110	80		Veneer
Hinge pin	1	25	3		Aluminium
Location pin	1	10	6	3	Hardwood

12

POTPOURRI BOX

otpourri is a collection of dried and scented flower petals and leaves. In Elizabethan stately homes, the potpourri maker was a man of great importance; sanitation was very primitive, to say the least, and this man's job was to prepare potpourri to be placed in bowls, so that the fragrance would mask the many unpleasant odours. More recently, and especially in Victorian times, no self-respecting housewife would fail to collect herbs and fragrant flowers for this purpose.

The use of potpourri has once again found favour in many houses, though not necessarily for the same reason!

There are many recipes for the home production of potpourri should you wish to experiment for yourself, but the choice of commercially produced potpourri is enormous and relatively cheap. Many potpourri boxes are made in India, and the permutations of design for such a container are endless and fascinating.

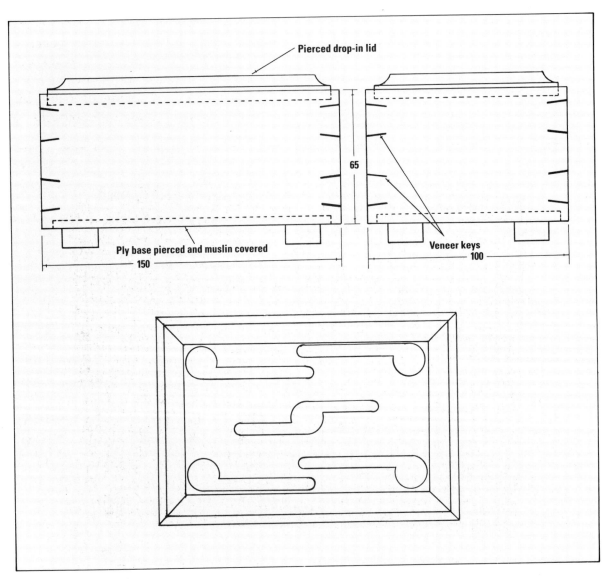

Fig 12.1 Front, end and plan views.

The sizes given are for guidance only, and can be altered depending on the volume required. I use a modification in the base to make the box more effective, but more of that later.

METHOD

Begin by selecting the wood for the outside of the box, either selecting an attractive timber or a timber that has its own distinctive aroma, such as cedar. The box shown in the photograph was made with English walnut and olive ash for the lid, which complements the walnut in a very warm manner.

As shown in Fig 12.1, a mitre joint, strengthened with veneer keys, is a good joint for this project, especially as the keys can contrast with the main carcase timber. The lid is a lose, drop-in type, and

the base is rebated and glued. If possible, keep the four sides as one piece of material, because small pieces are harder to work accurately.

The rebates for the lid and the bottom are best worked as soon as the wood is prepared to size. If you have a portable router, use a two-flute cutter; hold the wood in the vice and use the router fence to guide the cut. If you do not have a router, do not despair but cut the rebates by hand. It looks much better if the grain follows around the box, so mark out the front, followed by the first end, the back and finally the other end, allowing a small amount of waste between each piece. Label the ends of each piece with a mark on the outside, so that you can locate each piece in its proper place later.

The joints are now cut using any of the methods described in Chapter 3. Take care that opposite

Fig 12.2 The underside, showing piercing to allow air movement through the potpourri.

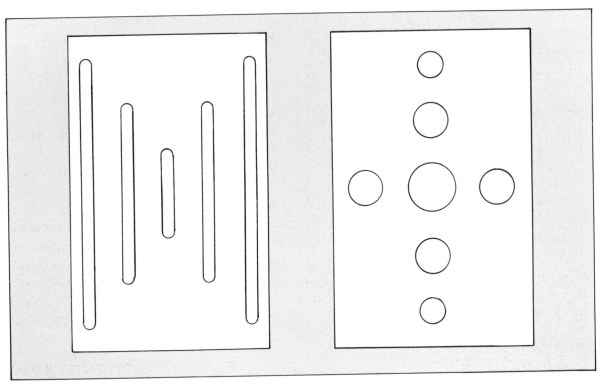

Fig 12.3 Alternative lid designs.

pieces finish exactly the same length, and adjust as necessary. Cramp up dry to check for any problems, and then glasspaper and polish the inside surfaces. Glue up, cramp and check the diagonals for square before setting aside to dry.

Veneer a small piece of 4mm ply on one side of the base. This is not normally a wise thing to do, as the ply could buckle under the strain of the extra thickness, but this will be remedied very shortly. Carefully cut to size and mark the centres for a series of 6mm holes before drilling them. When the box is finished, it will stand off the table on feet, which allows for a circulation of air to increase the effectiveness of the box (*see* Fig 12.2). The inside surface of the bottom should be covered with a suitable cloth, such as muslin, to ensure that the potpourri does not fall out.

Plane the wood for the lid to size so that it fits slightly loosely. The fretting of the top can be very simply cut, or can be made in a complicated design involving a great deal of work – be careful, however, that the fretting does not detract from the simplicity of the box.

The original box was designed as a wedding present for a musical niece, and the inspiration for the fretting came from musical notation. I have suggested two other designs in Fig 12.3, one of which relies only on drilled holes. No sizes are suggested, as so much will depend on your imagination, your facilities and the size of the box.

The router really comes into its own for this type of work; many cutters are available to produce different shapes, especially for edge mouldings. However, it should be emphasised that a router is not an essential tool for this work. Remember, it is quite a recent invention, and many of us managed for years with much simpler equipment!

When the glue has hardened on the joints, the box can be uncramped and marked out for the keys. Cut the slots dovetail fashion with a tenon

Fig 12.4 The veneer keys set on dovetail slopes of 1:6.

As the box will be quite fragile on the joints, it is worth making up a device to hold the carcase firmly while the key slots are cut. My frame has been used over a number of years, and is very simple to make from scrap material. Fig 4.7 gives the necessary information for its construction.

When the glue has hardened, saw off the excess key material and smoothing-plane the sides. Remember to plane 'into' the box, so that the keys are not splintered out. The carcase can now be glasspapered and polished.

The feet can be as simple or as complicated as you like. In the simplest form, four small blocks are glued to the bottom before the base is polished.

The longer this box is used, the more effective it will become, because the timber will gradually absorb the aroma from the potpourri, making it a potpourri in its own right (*see* Fig 12.5).

Fig 12.5 The inside of the box filled with potpourri.

saw, and fill the kerf with glued-in veneer (*see* Fig 12.4). Experiment to see how wide a kerf your chosen saw produces, and then glue together small pieces of veneer to produce the necessary thickness. If you want a thicker key, try cutting with two hacksaw blades held together in one frame.

SUGGESTED CUTTING LIST					
Lengths are gross, widths and thicknesses are net. All measurements in millimetres					
PART	NO. REQUIRED	LENGTH	WIDTH	THICK	MATERIAL
Front/back	2	160	65	12	Hardwood
Ends	2	120	65	12	Hardwood
Lid	1	150	100	14	Hardwood
Base	1	150	105	4	Plywood
Feet	4	18	18	9	Hardwood
Muslin	1	150	105		

13

SPICE BOXES

pices are by no means new to the kitchen, but in recent years their use appears to have undergone a welcome revival. There are many jars and containers available commercially for the storage of spices, and there is nothing to say that they should not be made from wood. Most spices, however, need to be kept in airtight containers; this can present problems for the woodworker, but care can overcome most of them.

It is best to make these boxes in pairs or fours. The wood must first be selected from a variety that will not contaminate the spice either by taste or smell: sycamore, beech or pear are all suitable. Steamed pear and spalted holly are used here.

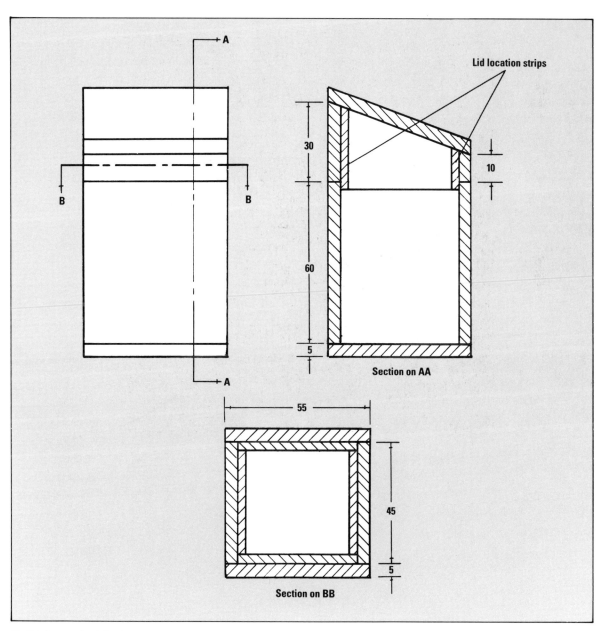

Fig 13.1 Front, end and plan views.

METHOD

Plane two strips to 55mm and 45mm wide respectively, and 5mm in thickness. The length is dependent on the size of the finished boxes, but for those shown in Fig 13.1, a length of 210mm will make two. The edges must be perfectly square and the sides parallel, as the wood is jointed with butt joints.

Should you intend making a number of these boxes, the use of a planing jig, as shown in Fig 4.9, would be advisable. Carefully glasspaper the inside surfaces, taking care to use a glasspaper block to avoid rounding off the outside edges.

Glue and cramp up to make a square tube, and leave to dry thoroughly. Plane the outside surfaces smooth, and mark out the length of each box. First square a knife line around one end, and then mark 110mm from the squared line on the proposed back surface.

Mark 90mm from the base line on the front side and then join up the front and back. Knife another set of lines 2mm away from these lines and then square another set of lines at the other end, 90mm away from the front side line.

Saw the tube into the two sections with a fine-cut saw, to prevent as much break-out of the fibres as possible. These surfaces now need to be planed perfectly flat with a finely set block plane, taking care that they are not damaged.

Select and plane suitable pieces of wood for the tops and bottoms, clean up the inside surfaces and glue them on. When set, plane the edges to the box sides and then square a knife line around 10mm below the bottom of the lid at the front. Cut to this line, and clean up the edges with a block plane in the same way as before.

The lid is held in place by four strips of 2mm thick wood glued to the inside of the lid; they protrude about 3mm, and the exposed edges are rounded off. Making the lid in this way ensures that a perfect fit is achieved between the top and the bottom.

Finally, glasspaper the entire outside surfaces and polish with the application of several coats of a good quality vegetable oil, such as peanut or olive (*see* Chapter 1).

The boxes can be labelled, either by carving in the name of the contents or by applying a set of printed labels.

SUGGESTED CUTTING LIST					
Lengths are gross, widths and thicknesses are net. All measurements in millimetres					
PART	NO. REQUIRED	LENGTH	WIDTH	THICK	MATERIAL
Front	1	95 (70)	55	5	Hardwood
Back	1	115 (90)	55	5	Hardwood
Sides	2	110 (85)	45	5	Hardwood
Base	1	55 (55)	55	5	Hardwood
Top	1	60 (60)	55	5	Hardwood
Lid location	2	30 (30)	45	3	Hardwood
Lid location	1	30 (30)	39	3	Hardwood
Lid location	1	15 (15)	39	3	Hardwood

14

TRADITIONAL PENCIL BOX

n recent years I have noticed a decline in the use of traditional pencil boxes by children in school. Instead, cases made from a variety of cloth and plastic materials are used. Too often pencils are broken because there is so little protection for them. These cases are frequently far too small for the number of pens and pencils that children carry.

For these reasons, the box shown in Fig 14.1 is larger than such boxes used to be, but is still of a reasonable size without being too bulky. As long as the box is long enough internally to accommodate the full length of its proposed contents, the dimensions can be altered at will.

The box shown is made from American black walnut produced in the UK, but almost any timber is suitable, although it does need to be reasonably hard to protect it from the rough treatment that it is likely to meet!

METHOD

Having chosen your timber, cut and plane it to 630mm × 60mm × 9mm. Work two grooves 5mm from each edge to 4mm deep, the bottom to a width of 3mm and the top to 4.5mm (see Fig 14.1). Mark out the length of each piece using a knife and a square: the long sides are 220mm and the ends

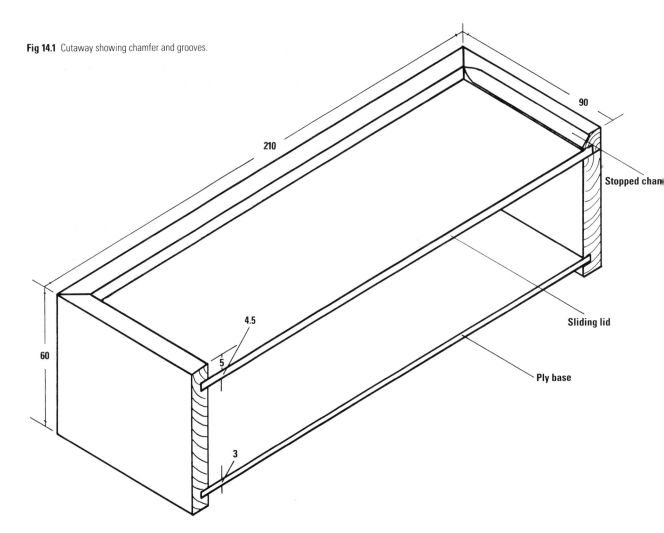

Fig 14.1 Cutaway showing chamfer and grooves.

90mm. Cut mitres on the end of each piece, and check that each pair is the same length. Plane off the top edge down to the bottom of the groove on one of the end pieces.

Make up plywood or select a manufactured ply for the base, and cut it to size. Dry-assemble the box with the base in place, to check that the box will glue up square and accurate. Sand and polish the inside surfaces and the base on both sides, and very carefully sand the now-exposed mitres on the open end. Take care not to remove too much or to round these mitres, as any gap created at this stage will show later.

Assemble and leave until the glue is set. Meanwhile prepare oversized plywood for the sliding top; this can either match the timber of the box or contrast with it. Very often the grain in the top of boxes follows the direction of the long side, so consider cross-banding it for a change.

Sand the top on both sides and cut it accurately to provide a sliding fit in the groove. It is as well to leave it overlength at this stage to provide a little leeway later. Cut a piece of wood to replace the section already removed, work a rebate to take the top and then cut mitres on the ends to make the new piece a tight fit.

Glue the end piece to the ply, taking care in getting it to its correct position. Cramp it up until the glue has set, and then work a stopped chamfer on the inside top edge of the end piece. Plane away any waste material and sand the end before polishing the entire lid.

If you have not already cleaned up the outside of the box, do so now before polishing. As a box of this type will take a lot of handling, use a hard-wearing polish such as Rustin's Clear Plastic Coating.

A box like this will be individual in any case, but you might consider inlaying or carving in the initials of the owner.

SUGGESTED CUTTING LIST					
Lengths are gross, widths and thicknesses are net. All measurements in millimetres					
PART	NO. REQUIRED	LENGTH	WIDTH	THICK	MATERIAL
Front/back	2	220	60	9	Hardwood
Ends	2	100	60	9	Hardwood
Top	1	210	80	4	Plywood
Top/bottom	4	210	80		Veneer
Bottom	1	210	80	3	Plywood
Finger grip	1	95	10	9	Hardwood

15

DESK PENCIL BOX

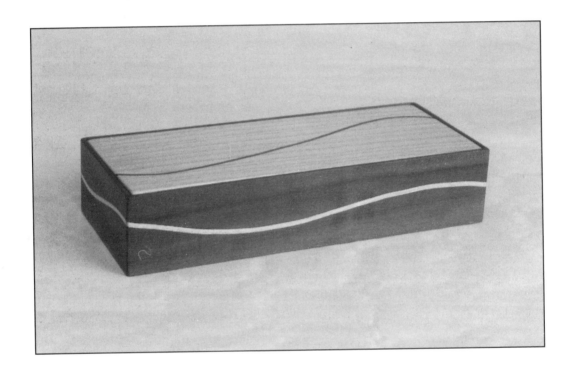

When designing anything, it is important to research everything to do with the project thoroughly. This is certainly true of this box: a new pencil is made to a standard length of 178mm, so the internal length of the box must be sufficient to hold the pencil. If the pencil box is to be made to hold ballpoint pens or overhead transparency pens, for instance, the measurements will need to be amended.

This is a basic box, which, as shown in the photographs and drawings, can be made into something quite different with just a little extra work and much care, especially when planning and cutting the curves.

As the top is set into the box frame and the bottom is either grooved in or rebated, as shown in Fig 15.1, it is advisable to work these rebates whilst the wood is in one length.

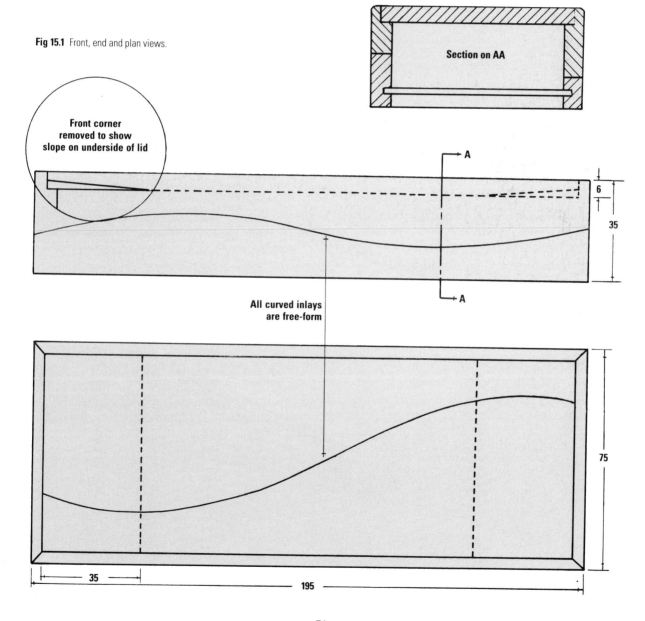

Fig 15.1 Front, end and plan views.

Section on AA

Front corner
removed to show
slope on underside of lid

All curved inlays
are free-form

A

A

6

35

75

35

195

METHOD

The inlaid design needs careful preparation, preferably by being drawn out full-size on paper. It is easier to temporarily join the front and back pieces together with double-sided tape, and then to transfer the curves to one surface using carbon paper from your drawing, or, if you are feeling more adventurous, straight on to the wood, using French curves. Strictly speaking, a section equal in width to the inlay needs to be removed, but I have found that for the small sizes used here, it is not strictly necessary.

The choice of sawing method will depend on personal skill and available tools: a jigsaw or bandsaw is ideal, as long as the process is unhurried and accurate. Provided that care has been taken in the sawing, nothing further will need to be done to the sawn edges; but if the cut is not accurate it will be necessary to trim the two edges to match, using a spokeshave. When satisfied with the match, the strips can be separated, taking care to label each part so it matches its partner.

The inlay should be in a contrasting timber; the original was made in planchonia (red bombway) and ash, but any contrasting combination will be suitable. Cut four strips of veneer for the inlay on each side, and spread glue on each to join together. Immediately glue each strip into place and cramp up the sides until the glue has cured.

The total length of the front and back can now be marked with a knife and square. Make up the end pieces now in a similar manner, taking care that the inlays will match up when the joints are finally cut.

The original was jointed with a half-lap joint, but a mitre would also be suitable. It is vital that the inlays line up all around the box, so adjust as

Fig 15.2 The chamfer on the underside of the lid.

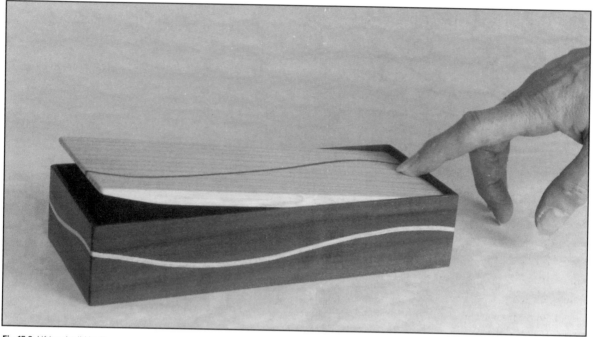

Fig 15.3 Lifting the lid by finger pressure.

necessary before cutting the joints.

When the joints have been cut, dry-cramp the box to check that all is in order, especially to check that the rebates line up in each corner. As the inside will be lined with a soft leather, sanding is only required on the rebate at the top. Glue up the box and check that it is square before putting it aside to cure.

Plywood for the base can be prepared and glued in when the box has set. The outside surfaces now need to be cleaned up and the grain sealed.

Prepare the material for the lid in the same way as the sides, and glue up with the laminates in position. When set, plane the lid to thickness and fit to size in the rebate (*see* Fig 15.2).

The underside now has to be planed to half the end thickness for a length of 35mm. When in place, check that the lid rises properly by applying slight downward pressure near one end (*see* Fig 15.3).

Clean up and polish the lid and the box. Finally, cut leather to size for the linings and glue them in, using Copydex or some similar adhesive.

SUGGESTED CUTTING LIST					
Lengths are gross, widths and thicknesses are net. All measurements in millimetres					
PART	**NO. REQUIRED**	**LENGTH**	**WIDTH**	**THICK**	**MATERIAL**
Front/back	2	205	40	8	Hardwood
Ends	2	85	40	8	Hardwood
Top	1	200	75	8	Hardwood
Base	1	200	75	4	Plywood
Inlays					Small pieces of veneer
Linings					Leather

16

SWIVEL BOX

wivel boxes are great fun to make. They can provide you with headaches, but generally only when you do not plan properly.

The box shown in the chapter-opening photograph has an overall size of 230mm × 130mm × 40mm, the measurements given in the suggesting cutting list, although much will depend on available material. It was made using spalted sycamore for the tray and the end infill, and yew for the top and bottom. The top was made from two pieces of yew that were joined together to create the line of sapwood in the middle of the board. I have made very successful boxes of quite different sizes, even using some Douglas fir salvaged from an old church pew.

It is important to make sure that the timber used is dry and stable, or you will possibly have trouble with the wood warping, which will make the tray bind on the top or bottom.

METHOD

Prepare the timber for the tray by planing it to size, paying particular attention to thicknessing, to ensure that the top and bottom surfaces are parallel (*see* Fig 16.1). Mark out the recess and prepare to cut it out in one of several ways.

1 The easiest way is to make a template with an electric router as described in Chapter 5 and rout out the waste, leaving about 5mm in the base.
2 If you have a bench drill, the waste can be drilled out and the edges carefully trimmed back with a chisel. First, drill around the outside edge to give a depth leaving about 6mm for the base, and then remove the remainder, using as large a drill as possible. Ideally you should use a saw-tooth machine centre bit for this, or else an ordinary jobber's bit (*see* Fig 16.2).

The bottom will need to be levelled and flattened, either with the good old hand router or by getting a local engineering company to re-grind a twist bit to produce a flat end, making a flat-bottomed hole possible (*see* Fig 16.3).
3 The tray can be successfully made in two parts. Remove the centre of the tray completely by sawing it out, and then glue a 5mm thick base on to its bottom.

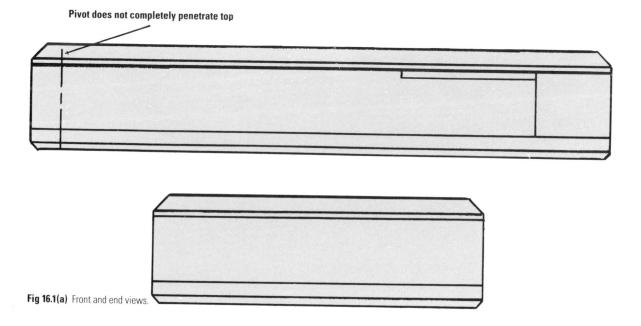

Pivot does not completely penetrate top

Fig 16.1(a) Front and end views.

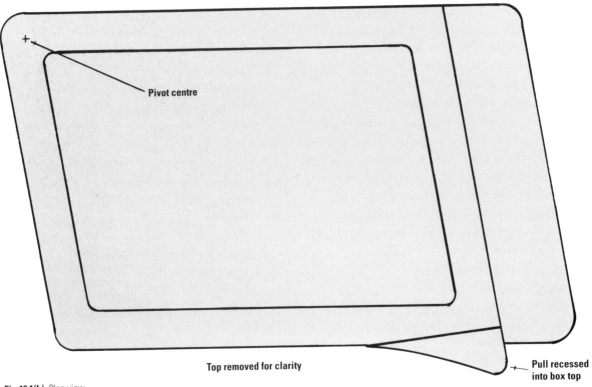

Pivot centre

Top removed for clarity

Pull recessed into box top

Fig 16.1(b) Plan view.

Fig 16.2 From left to right: sawtooth machine bit, Forstner bit, jobber's twist bit and modified twist bit.

The end infill acts as a spacer for the tray and needs to be fractionally thicker than the tray, so that the tray can swing with relative ease. This piece needs to be cleaned up and polished on the inside edge only. It is then glued to the prepared base and left until the glue has set.

Mark out the centre of the pivot pin on the tray, ensuring that there is plenty of wood around it. The pin is made from 6mm dowel, so drill this size in the tray for the moment. Locate the tray in its position on the base and, using the hole in the tray, drill into and through the base material.

Glue on the top, but only to the infill piece, and, when the glue has set, locate the tray in position. Drill into the top, stopping about 3mm from the outside.

Test the fit with a dowel in place, and adjust the thickness of the tray to provide a slack fit. (You may have to slightly enlarge the hole in the tray, but this is unlikely.) The outside surfaces can now be planed and chamfers worked on the top and bottom (*see* Fig 16.1) before glasspapering and polishing.

The pin can now be glued in place, but make careful preparations first. Work a chamfer on the top end and cut a few grooves, to allow air to escape into both ends.

Put a small amount of glue into the top hole, and push the dowel in from the bottom before spreading a small amount of glue on the protruding dowel. Finally, push it in fully and test

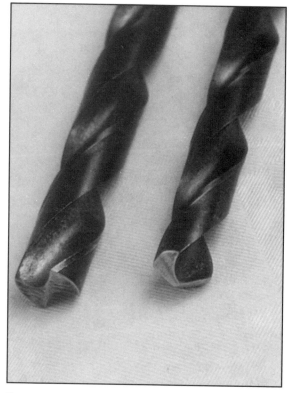

Fig 16.3 The twist bit on the left was modified from a standard twist bit on the right.

for movement. Provided you have used the minimum amount of glue necessary, you will have no worries about the tray sticking to the top or bottom, but check frequently while the glue sets by pushing the tray in and out.

As a final and luxurious touch, line the inside of the tray with some soft leather (*see* page 28).

SUGGESTED CUTTING LIST					
Lengths are gross, widths and thicknesses are net. All measurements in millimetres					
PART	NO. REQUIRED	LENGTH	WIDTH	THICK	MATERIAL
Top/bottom	2	230	130	10	Hardwood
End infill	1	130	30	25	Hardwood
Tray	1	210	130	25	Hardwood
Tray pull	1	65	25	5	Hardwood
Pivot	1	6 dia.			Dowel
Linings					Leather

17

STUDENT'S STATIONERY COMPENDIUM

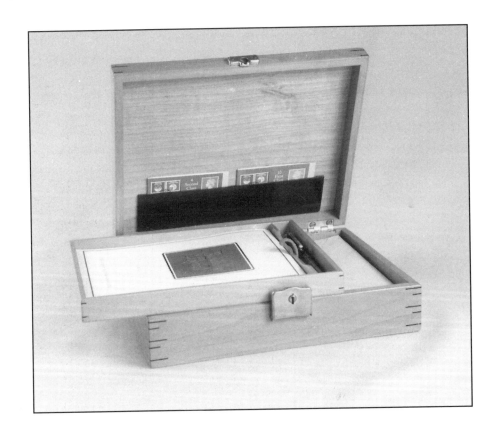

My three children have all gone to college, and have all been told to write to Mum, Grandma, Uncle, Aunt, etc. What better than to supply them with the necessary equipment – pad, stamps, envelopes and pen space – neatly stowed in a lightweight box?

Beware of writing pad sizes, as they seem to be a law unto themselves; buy a pad and envelopes *first*, and make the box to suit the size. The sizes given in the suggested cutting list are for a pad measuring 178mm × 137mm and matching envelopes, so alter them to suit your own pad.

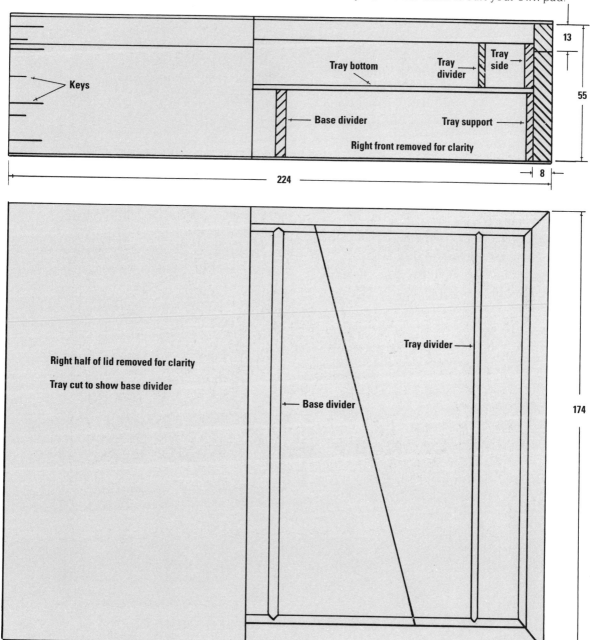

Fig 17.1 Front and plan views.

METHOD

The original is made of steamed pear: this timber is a delight to use, producing a good finish with very little trouble. As it is a dense, close-grained timber, it is relatively hard, yet still quite light in weight.

Plane your selected timber of 800mm long to 55mm × 8mm. As there is no rebating to do, one long piece is not a necessity, though I prefer it to be so to allow the grain to follow around the box.

Prepare a strip of the same timber 970mm long to 27mm × 3mm, and glue this to the bottom of the main piece. This strip will eventually support the inner tray. The small remainder will be a divider in the base of the box (see Fig 17.1).

Mark off the front and back to 224mm and the ends to 174mm, allowing waste between each piece. Cut mitre joints on each end and check that each end joins satisfactorily. Mark out the centre on the insides of the front and back and mark a

Fig 17.2 The veneer keys.

double mitre into it to half the divider's thickness, using a saw and chisel to remove the mitre waste.

Dry-cramp the box, cut the divider piece to length and double-mitre its ends to fit into the

Fig 17.3 Stamp holders shown from the back.

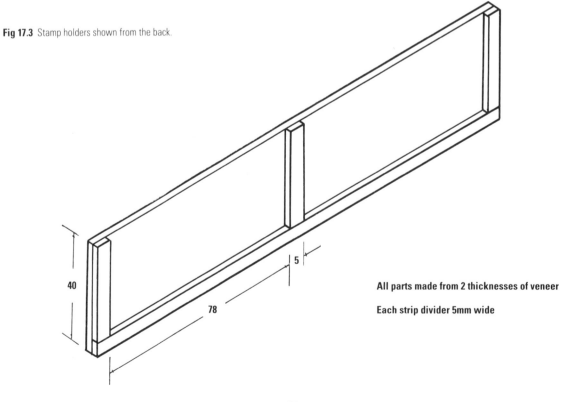

40

78

5

All parts made from 2 thicknesses of veneer

Each strip divider 5mm wide

mating parts. Clean up the inside surfaces and glue up the box.

The veneer keys are now worked on the corners. Instead of making them all the same, mark out alternative keys to lengths of 8mm and 14mm, as shown in Fig 17.2. Leave sufficient space between numbers 2 and 3 from the top edge to allow for cutting the lid later. For another change, have the keys parallel to the top.

Cramp the box in the holder, as described on page 33, and cut the key slots with a fine saw. Cut and glue in the keys, making sure that each one beds down fully to the bottom of each slot. Glue up three sheets of veneer to make a ply for the top, base and inner tray base.

Measure the inside dimensions of the box, and write them down.

Smooth the inside surfaces with glasspaper before gluing the top and bottom on.

The inside tray can be made while the glue is setting, so prepare a piece 750mm × 18mm × 5mm and one piece 160mm × 18mm × 3mm. Mark out to the sizes already noted, and cut mitre joints on the corners. Cut in the divider 18mm from one end in the same way as for the box divider and shape the top edge of the divider as shown in Fig 17.1. Glasspaper the inside surfaces of the tray and both sides of the divider. Glue up the tray, then cut and fit the keys when the glue is set.

Plane down the top and bottom flush with the box sides, and glasspaper all surfaces smooth. Mark the line to form the lid with a marking gauge. Using a fine saw, cut around the box and carefully plane the edges smooth, ensuring a good match.

Mark out the hinge recesses for 18mm hinges and fit them. Fit a brass box lock to the surface of the front edge, and then remove both hinges and the lock.

Make up the holders to contain books of postage stamps – *see* Fig 17.3. This is done by gluing two veneers 190mm × 45mm together. You will also need two strips, one of 190mm × 7mm and one of 120mm × 7mm, each two veneers thick. When set and planed in width to 40mm, 5mm and 5mm respectively, glue the strips to the back of the larger piece in the form of a letter E, allowing 78mm between each 'arm'. Smooth up and glue this assembly to the inside back edge of the lid.

Polish the box to suit your own requirements, and finally refit the hinges and lock.

SUGGESTED CUTTING LIST

Lengths are gross, widths and thicknesses are net. All measurements in millimetres

PART	NO. REQUIRED	LENGTH	WIDTH	THICK	MATERIAL
Front/back	2	235	55	8	Hardwood
Ends	2	180	55	8	Hardwood
Top/bottom	2	230	185	2	Plywood
Tray supports	2	215	27	3	Hardwood
Tray supports	3	170	27	3	Hardwood
Tray front/back	2	215	18	5	Hardwood
Tray ends	2	165	18	5	Hardwood
Tray divider	1	165	18	3	Hardwood
Tray bottom	1	215	165	2	Plywood
Stamp holder	2	180	40		Veneer
Stamp holder	2	310	5		Veneer
Hinges	2	18	Butt		Brass

18

HIS AND HERS
TRIANGULAR
JEWELLERY BOXES

ewellery boxes tend to be regarded as the domain of the female, but more men are now wearing items of jewellery and therefore need a convenient storage box. As they tend to have fewer items, the 'His' box does not need to be so deep and probably does not need the extra space provided by a loose tray. Triangular boxes provide a degree of interest and challenge in their production, making them a pleasant change from the more usual rectangular variety.

Use a good quality decorative hardwood – British or American walnut is ideal. A contrast is needed for the lid inlay, and here the choice is wide open: try a burr or quarter-cut veneer.

METHOD

The timber should be planed to the proposed width and thickness in one length. Rebate the top edge to a depth of 4.5mm, and work a 3mm groove 3mm above the bottom. The length is marked out for each side; leave a small amount of waste between each piece.

Set a sliding bevel to 30°, using a good quality set square as a template (*see* Fig 18.1), and use a knife to mark each end of the three pieces with this setting. Label each end consecutively so that the grain will follow around the box when it is assembled.

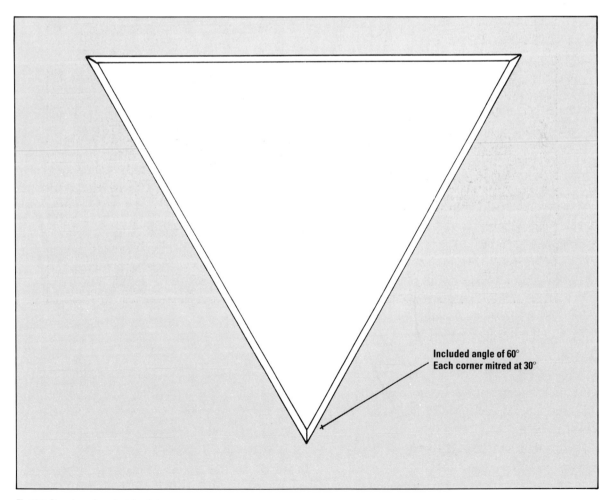

Included angle of 60°
Each corner mitred at 30°

Fig 18.1 Plan view of regular triangle box.

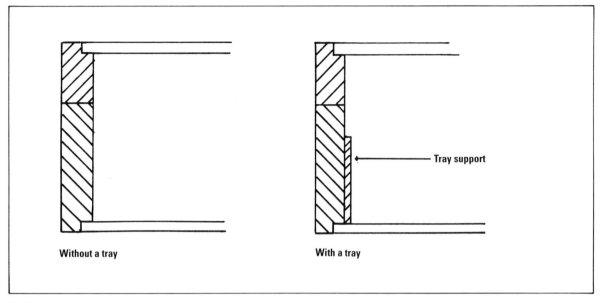

Without a tray

With a tray

Tray support

Fig 18.2 Box side with and without tray support.

In the case of 'Hers', a strip of wood needs to be prepared and glued on to the inside surface; this piece will support the drop-in tray when all is finished (*see* Fig 18.2). It will need to be no thicker than 3mm, and is glued on so that its bottom edge is at the top of the base groove.

Saw slightly on the waste side of each knife line and then very carefully plane to the line, using a finely set block plane. Check that all joints assemble correctly before the next stage. Make up the base piece for the box in whatever way you prefer, clean it up and polish on the inside only.

Cut the base to size, glasspaper and polish and wait for the fun to begin, as gluing up a triangle can be very interesting. By far the best 'cramp' for this purpose is a large rubber band, so visit your local car tyre depot and cadge a discarded car inner tube. It is a good idea to have a selection of different sized tubes, to provide a wide range of cramp sizes.

Cut the tube into bands of varying widths and use one of them to cramp up your triangle. Try it without glue at first, to get used to handling an awkward set of components. When you are happy

that all is in order, apply glue and elastic pressure and leave until the glue has set.

Meanwhile, veneer a piece of 3mm or 4mm plywood with decorative timber on each side, and when ready mark out and fit it into the lid. A word of warning: as the box will not yet have been cut to form the lid, do not push it right home! When you are satisfied with the fit, clean up the underside only and glue it into the rebate.

Plane the outside surfaces and the protruding edges of the lid before using a marking gauge to mark the lid depth. Use a very fine saw and cut around the line, taking great care to saw accurately to the line. Plane these edges with a block plane until they line up properly and accurately.

Cramp the lid and box together on the back edge, and mark out the position for 25mm solid drawn brass butt hinges. Set these into both the lid and the box, working carefully to achieve a good line-up of box and lid when the box is closed.

Fit the hinges first with steel screws of the same type and size as the intended brass ones – this will ensure that the head of the softer brass screw is not easily damaged when it is fitted.

The loose tray for the 'Hers' box is made from 3mm thick material for the sides and a plywood of three layers of veneer for its base. Decide on the way that you want to arrange the tray, or even whether more than one tray is needed, and cut your material accordingly.

A simple butt joint is all that is required at the corners and for joining on to the base. Spring cramps are very useful for this operation. Remember to clean up all inside surfaces before you glue up.

Glasspaper all unpapered surfaces and polish.

SUGGESTED CUTTING LIST

Lengths are gross, widths and thicknesses are net. All measurements in millimetres

PART	NO. REQUIRED	LENGTH	WIDTH	THICK	MATERIAL
(His)					
Sides	3	210	50	9	Hardwood
Top/bottom	3	400	170		Veneer
Hinges	2	25			Brass butt
(Hers)					
Sides	3	210	60	9	Hardwood
Top/bottom	3	400	170		Veneer
Tray sides	1	430	12	3	Hardwood
Tray bottom	1	300	150		Veneer
Tray supports	3	170	25	3	Hardwood
Hinges	2	25			Brass butt

19

MUSICAL BOX

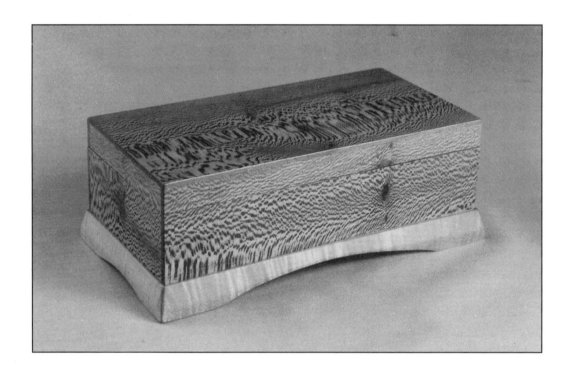

Musical boxes have been popular for years – and rightly so: they have entertained and kept children amused for hours by the beautiful sound quality and the magic of music beginning when the lid is lifted.

The original musical boxes were made as novelty items by clockmakers in the eighteenth century. They were generally very small, and were often fitted into walking stick handles or in tiny snuff boxes. Early in the nineteenth century, David LeCoultre is credited with developing the first large movement capable of producing a range of tunes.

As now, the movement was clockwork powered; a cylinder with protruding steel studs revolved and produced musical sounds by the pins striking against a steel comb arrangement. The teeth of the comb were of different lengths and were tuned to a musical scale. In time other designs were produced, some of which could play a large

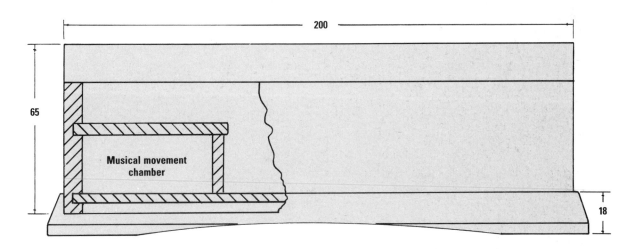

Parts of front and end removed for clarity

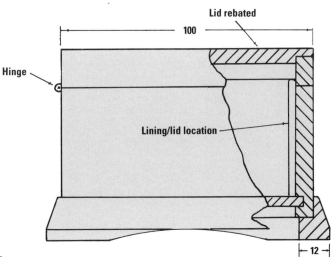

Fig 19.1 Front and end views.

number of popular tunes. Many of these early boxes were very ornately made, using a variety of exotic veneers, and now command very high prices at auction.

For this box, select timber from stock with quarter-cut figure. The original was made of London plane, which when quarter-cut is known as lacewood. This timber is very beautiful, and is probably the most marked English timber when so cut; however, when it is sawn through and through, it is exceptionally dull in colour and pattern!

A piece 640mm long finished to 60mm × 8mm is required to complete the outside, together with a piece 210mm long planed to 100mm × 6mm for the top. The bottom is a piece of 4mm ply decorated with a veneer of your choice.

METHOD

Cut the joints of your choice on the corners, bearing in mind that the bottom will be grooved into the sides. As the movement will be at one end, prepare the plywood panel and mark out the position of the fixing screws which will hold it in place. Drill these, together with a hole for the key and winding spindle.

The mechanism needs to be isolated from the rest of the box cavity, so cut a housing joint in the front and back to hold the divider, making sure that the top is about 6mm above the top of the mechanism (see Fig 19.1).

As there are several different types of movement, I have not detailed the mechanism

Fig 19.2 The musical movement compartment and a small 'secret' compartment.

needed to stop and start the movement when the lid is lifted, especially as most movements are supplied with fitting instructions. Suffice it to say that it will be necessary at this stage to make provision for this action. Fig 19.2 shows a movement in place and a 'secret compartment'.

You should now provide a lid for the chamber; this should be a good fit, but one in which the lid can be removed at a later time if necessary. It need only be about 4mm thick.

Glue up the box after polishing the underside of the base. Clean up the top edge and prepare the lid material before cutting a rebate around its edge. When you are satisfied with the fit, clean it up and glue it in place. When set, plane the outside surfaces of the box and mark out the lid cut-off point with a marking gauge. Cut around the line and then plane the sawn edges for a snug fit.

At this stage I lined the box with cedar. I used cedar because this timber has a very pleasant aroma which will be smelt every time the lid is lifted. Fit so that the lining is flush on the back edge, but allow it to stand proud by about 3mm on the sides and front.

Mark out and sink 25mm solid drawn brass butt hinges on the back edge. This type of box is set off beautifully when a plinth is added to the bottom edges, which also has the benefit of making sure that the key is hidden and above the surface on which the box will stand. I like subtle contrasts, and so I made mine from sycamore worked to 18mm high by 10mm thick (see Fig 19.1).

Cut mitres on the corners after working a rebate on the inside top surface. Shape the underside on each piece so that only the corners rest on the surface, and work the vertical surfaces into a bevel or other suitable section. Glue the plinth on, taking care that excess glue does not squeeze out.

Finally, polish the box with a suitable polish such as Rustin's Clear Plastic Coating.

SUGGESTED CUTTING LIST					
Lengths are gross, widths and thicknesses are net. All measurements in millimetres					
PART	NO. REQUIRED	LENGTH	WIDTH	THICK	MATERIAL
Front/back	2	210	55	8	Hardwood
Ends	2	105	55	8	Hardwood
Top	1	210	100	8	Hardwood
Base	1	200	100	4	Plywood
Mouldings	2	215	18	10	Hardwood
Mouldings	2	115	18	10	Hardwood
Hinges	2	18			Brass butt
Musical movement	1				

20

PENTAGONAL BOX

Multi-sided boxes, those with five or more sides, provide interest in appearance and diversity in construction. There is no reason why a box should have just four sides – there are times when three, five, six, seven or whatever might be better. In the same way, it would be very boring to use only one timber when a craftsman has the opportunity of using many of the world's beautiful timbers. Sometimes it is good to be different!

A little knowledge of Euclidean geometry, to accurately work out the corner angles, will be useful for this box. However, this is not so necessary if a mitre saw is available, although the knowledge is still very desirable, if only to have a fair idea of what is needed.

All regular shapes having sides of the same length can be fitted into a circle. Each side, when joined to the centre, forms an isosceles triangle (*see* Fig 20.1). This means that the two sides adjacent to the centre are equal in length. In order to work out the necessary angle, follow the following procedure.

1 Divide 360° by the number of sides.
2 Subtract this answer from 180° and divide by 2.

This will give the angle at the corner of each triangle.

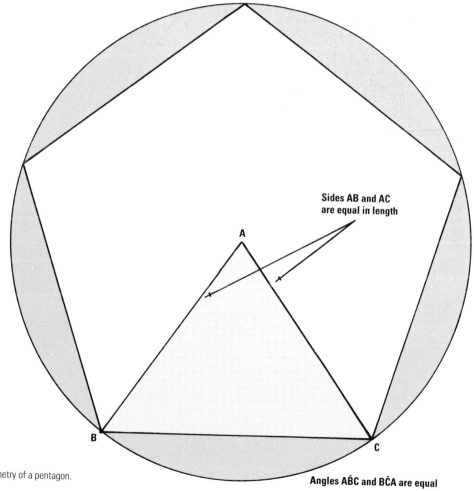

Sides AB and AC are equal in length

Fig 20.1 Geometry of a pentagon.

Angles AB̂C and BĈA are equal

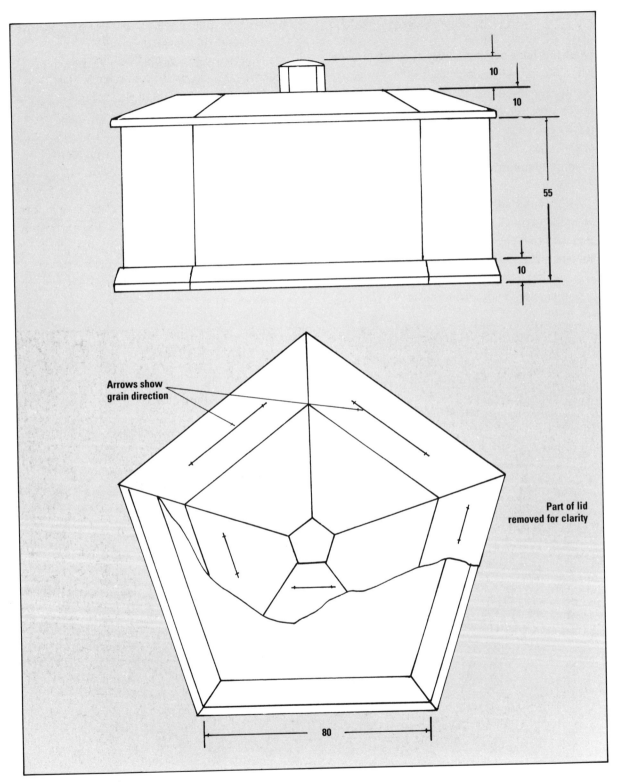

10

10

55

10

Arrows show grain direction

Part of lid removed for clarity

80

Fig 20.2 Front and plan views.

METHOD

When making a pentagonal box with 80mm long sides, the following sequence is used.

1 $360 \div 5 = 72°$, this being the angle at the centre ($<$BAC).

2 $180 - 72 = 108° \div 2 = 54°$, this being the angle needed to cut the ends of the sides.

If a mitre saw is not available, set an angle of 54° on a sliding bevel. Mark the length of each piece and then mark the angle. The bottom can be glued straight on to the base when assembled or set into a rebate: if the latter, cut the rebate at this stage. Cut and fit the joints, paying particular attention to the marking lines – it is essential that all five sides are the same length (*see* Fig 20.2).

Clean up the insides before gluing the sides together. This stage will give problems that do not exist with four-sided boxes! None of the traditional cramps will be of much use, and even the web cramp will give problems because of the tendency of the glue to impregnate the web. Fortunately the motor trade provides the necessary cramp in the form of plastic ties. These are now used instead of jubilee clips when rubber gaiters are fitted to cover such things as universal joints. Although they are not individually long enough, they can be joined together to make a versatile cramp which makes the task of gluing up five sides very easy indeed (*see* Fig 20.3).

Fig 20.3 Plastic ties cramping the glued sides.

The drop-in lid will look very attractive if it is constructed in segments which are glued with a contrasting veneer line between them. Cut the triangular pieces to the same angle of 54°. The outside edges will need to be slightly longer, to provide an overhang to the box. These segments are glued up in the same manner as the sides, preferably on a flat surface protected with paper.

While the glue is setting, prepare and veneer a piece of plywood for the base; glue it on the bottom of the box when the glue has set.

Plane up the top and provide a location system, either by working a rebate around the underside of the lid or by cutting small strips to glue on the lid, again using a 54° angle for the ends (this latter method is somewhat fiddly and time-consuming). The top of the lid can be tapered towards the edges by carefully planing with a smoothing plane.

This type of lid always leads to some controversy – some people prefer to add a knob of some kind, and others are adamant that none should be fitted. Any knob used should be kept as simple as possible, but must fit into the scheme of the box: I decided that my box would be better with a knob, and a simple pentagonal shape matched the box (see Fig 20.2).

A box of this type can also feature a small moulding around the outside bottom edge. Mouldings need not be ornate as in days gone by, but can be just as effective when cut as a rectangle with the front edge bevelled.

Whatever your choice, prepare the moulding as one piece; it can be rebated or planted straight on to the sides. Cut each piece to length and glue the pieces on to the sanded but unpolished box. Remove all surplus glue and allow to dry before final sanding and polishing.

The inside can be finished by making up a padded base covered in a material such as velour, and gluing it in position.

SUGGESTED CUTTING LIST					
Lengths are gross, widths and thicknesses are net. All measurements in millimetres					
PART	NO. REQUIRED	LENGTH	WIDTH	THICK	MATERIAL
Sides	5	90	55	9	Hardwood
Base	1	135	135	3	Plywood
Tops	5	90	65	9	Hardwood
Knob	1	15	15	12	Hardwood
Veneer	Offcuts				

21

TEA CADDY

It would appear that tea caddies are becoming things of the past. Looking around the shelves in supermarkets, it seems that more people are buying teabags than packets of loose tea. What a shame if the tea caddy were to disappear, to become only a collectable item.

The word 'caddy' comes from the Malay word *kati*, which means a measure of tea, about 1¼lbs (0.56kg). Caddies were developed in the early to mid-1700s to cater for the new craze of tea drinking by the upper classes, as only they could afford the high cost of the product. The caddies were initially made from porcelain, but later silver, gold and very ornate wooden caddies came into fashion.

Because tea was so expensive, locks were fitted to the caddies to prevent pilfering by the servants, and the key was carefully guarded by the lady of the house!

Chippendale and Sheraton were among the well-known furniture makers who designed and made caddies to complement their work. These old caddies now command very high prices at auction, and are very collectable.

I like tea and I like good handmade items that add to the quality of life, so what better than a modern tea caddy? It is very difficult to design such a traditional thing as this, because tastes differ so much. Should it be simple and plain, or ornate? There is a happy medium, but decoration must be left to the individual, so I will only describe a basic caddy, together with some suggestions for decoration.

Tea is a very particular product, and some points need to be mentioned so that the flavour is not spoilt in storage. The choice of timber is important: it must have no smell and must not impart any taste to the tea. Sycamore is an ideal timber for this project, especially so if the timber is rippled, as in a violin back.

The container needs to be reasonably airtight, to enhance the shelf life of the product. Tea is transported around the world in boxes and bags

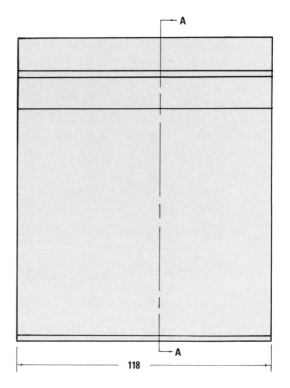

All wood 6mm thick

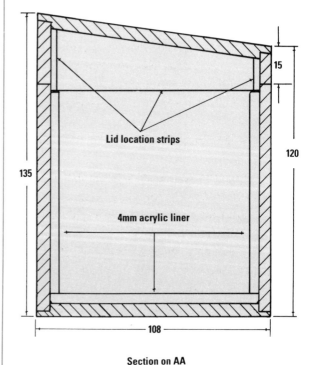

Fig 21.1 Front and end views.

lined with aluminium; this can be done on the inside of this caddy, but I made a separate liner from acrylic.

The first thing to do is to decide on the quantity of tea that the caddy is expected to hold. Tea is sold in packets of 125g and 250g. Measuring these and multiplying the three dimensions together will give the volumetric capacity needed. It will then only need to be made to suit your purpose. However, don't forget that it will have to accommodate your hand! The sizes quoted and shown in Fig 21.1 will hold a little more than 250g.

METHOD

Have the grain of the timber running vertically. The joint is a simple rebate with the sides glued into it. Plane all pieces to 6mm thick, the two sides to 109mm wide and the front and back to 118mm (*see* Fig 21.1). It is easier to do this as two strips so that the rebates can be cut at the same time. Rebate strips to a depth of 3mm and to 6mm wide. Check that the sides fit in accurately, and use a shoulder plane to adjust the rebate where necessary.

Cut the front, back and sides to 145mm in length. Smooth the inside surfaces with glasspaper until all is very clean and smooth. Glue up the box and cramp until the glue has set, remembering to check the assembly for 90° in the corners.

The bottom end now needs to be cut flat and square to the vertical. Scribe a line around, using a square and a knife, and plane to the line. Put a block of scrap wood behind the box in the vice to stop the timber breaking out, and then carefully plane to the line, using a finely set plane. Remember that at this stage the box will still be a little fragile, so perhaps a loose but neat-fitting block slid into place would help. Whatever you do, proceed with caution!

Now plane up a piece of timber for the base, making it slightly oversize to allow for planing when assembled. It is best to rebate this in: mark out the rebate by offering the box to the wood and scribing around the inside with a very sharp pencil. Mark the depth of the rebate to 3mm, using a marking gauge, and check that all is in order with the marking out. If you have a rebate plane, it can be set to cut to 3mm, with a width of cut as required.

Remember to use the small knife cutter when you are cutting across the grain; a router can also be used. If you have neither, cut to the line with a tenon saw and remove the waste with a chisel, finishing off with a shoulder plane.

Check the base for fit, and amend if necessary. Smooth up the inside surface and glue it in, holding with cramps for as long as is needed.

Mark off the total length of 135mm at the back and 120mm at the front with a knife and square, and then join up the lines with a knife and straightedge. Mark off the lid 104mm from the bottom in a similar manner. Cut the sloping edge first, and then carefully cut the lid from the box (*see* Fig 21.1).

Make the top in a manner similar to the base, but cut the front and back edges to the rebates to accommodate the slopes of the lid. Again, make the lid slightly bigger, to permit planing when finally assembled. Fit in the same way as the base.

Prepare wood to 3mm thick for the location strips in the lid with the grain also running up and down the box. When these are glued in, they will create a good airtight fit.

The inner lining is made with acrylic, a modern plastic material which is easy to use. If you have difficulty in obtaining this material, a visit to a local signmaker will probably solve the problem. The acrylic will have a covering paper on both surfaces to protect it from scratching, as this type of plastic is soft and easily damaged; leave the paper on for as long as possible.

Make the liner to be a good sliding fit within the caddy (*see* Fig 21.1). Remember, however, that too tight a fit will produce an airlock, making it

Fig 21.2 The chacahuante inlay makes a dramatic contrast with the figured sycamore.

impossible for the liner's full entry. Cut the material to size using a handsaw; it will dull the edge, so the best saw to use is a hacksaw. This material is brittle, so take care: when sawing, cramp it firmly to the end of the bench, using a protecting block to prevent surface damage.

Begin by cutting the base to be a sliding fit inside the box, taking care that you do not make it so tight that it will not come out. Prepare the sides to size, making sure that all adjoining edges are square.

Smear a thin layer of adhesive on to the bottom edge of one side and to the abutting edge of the bottom surface, and align the two pieces at once. The solvent action will begin immediately, and will be set within a few minutes. The correct adhesive to use is Tensol No. 6, but a very good substitute is Bison Hard Plastic Adhesive. As these are solvents, you should work in a well-ventilated area and make sure that the adhesive is not applied to any surfaces other than the intended ones!

Repeat the operation for the two adjacent sides and finally the last side. Place the liner aside for the chemical process to cure fully, and then remove any protruding edges with a plane and glasspaper. Acrylic can be planed accurately to size, using a finely set smoothing plane with a slicing action.

Acrylic can be papered with glasspaper or emery cloth, but work through the grades until you are using 400 grit. This also applies to the corners, to ease the passage into the caddy casing by providing an air escape passage.

Avoid scratching any part of the surface, as marks are difficult to remove. If you have access to a buffing wheel, this will polish the lining beautifully. Sadly, not many of us will have this luxury, so elbow grease will have to do. When you have finished papering, apply a good quality metal polish with a soft cloth, and keep burnishing the surface. It does not take long, but only perseverance will produce the results.

Decoration can now be worked if wanted. My original caddy was made from a beautiful piece of figured sycamore, and so needed very little extra ornamentation. However, I did cut two grooves 3mm wide and 2mm deep on the top and front (*see* Fig 21.2), and filled them with strips of chacahuante, a beautiful red timber from Mexico.

A pattern of circles could also be recessed into the timber and filled with a contrasting timber. These need not necessarily be finished flush, but could also be recessed, or even protruding with a rounded surface. Use any decoration with restraint and care, especially as the more simple the pattern, the less it detracts from the qualities of the wood.

Finally, clean up and polish the outside surfaces of the caddy. Not every polish can be used, because of the problems with the material already mentioned. Whatever is used, it must not contain chlorophenols, as these tend to degrade into chloroanisoles, which will taint the tea. A very good polish to use is Rustin's Clear Plastic Coating; but **apply this only to the outside surfaces.**

SUGGESTED CUTTING LIST					
Lengths are gross, widths and thicknesses are net. All measurements in millimetres					
PART	NO. REQUIRED	LENGTH	WIDTH	THICK	MATERIAL
Front	1	115	116	7	Hardwood
Back	1	130	116	7	Hardwood
Sides	2	130	102	7	Hardwood
Top	1	120	110	7	Hardwood
Base	1	120	108	7	Hardwood
Lid locations	2	90	30	3	Hardwood
Lid location back	1	110	30	3	Hardwood
Lid location front	1	110	17	3	Hardwood
Front/back liners	2	90	100	4	Acrylic
Sides liners	2	90	85	4	Acrylic
Base liner	1	110	95	4	Acrylic

22

ROUTER CUTTER BOX

It would be very interesting to conduct a survey about the storage of router bits. I suspect that most are kept in baccy tins, plastic containers that have found their way out of the kitchen, and various other types of containers that are no longer needed for their original purposes. Router bits are expensive and are easily damaged when not stored properly; a good storage container for them is a very good investment, both in time and cash.

Individual needs must be taken into acount as far as the size and layout of this box is concerned, but some general points should be made:

- the base needs to be made from a hard wood, to prevent the wear of holes from constant use.
- it also needs to be heavy, to give stability when the lid is open.
- allow sufficient space between bits to allow for their removal.
- make the box too big for present use, in order to provide storage for extra cutters later.
- provide space for spanners, Allen keys, and other frequently used items.
- for the box, use a timber that will withstand the knocks it will inevitably receive.
- remember that some bits are much longer than others!
- plan the layout of the inside on paper.

METHOD

Having selected and planed the chosen timber to size, mark out and cut suitable joints for the corners. Clean up the inside surfaces, glue the box together and check that it is square. When the glue has cured, plane the top and bottom edges flat and true.

The base needs to be at least 18mm and preferably 21mm in thickness, two-thirds of which needs to be rebated into the box. Before gluing the base into the box, it will be necessary to mark out the positions for the bits and sundry items. Bear in mind that once the holes are drilled it is too late to change your mind, so check at this point to see that the layout is sensible, and amend it if necessary. Drill all the holes fractionally oversize to allow for swelling of the timber during damp periods in the workshop.

Items such as spanners will need to be held in some way. The obvious method is to rout out a shape to suit and then sink a couple of magnets flush with the surface, to hold the item in place.

Clean up and polish the top surface of the base and glue it into position, together with the top of the box.

Plane and glasspaper the entire box and finally polish with either Danish oil or Rustin's Clear Plastic Coating; either will produce a hard finish.

SUGGESTED CUTTING LIST

Lengths are gross, widths and thicknesses are net. All measurements in millimetres

PART	NO. REQUIRED	LENGTH	WIDTH	THICK	MATERIAL
Front	1	180	75	9	Hardwood
Back	1	180	90	9	Hardwood
Ends	2	115	90	9	Hardwood
Top	1	180	115	6	Hardwood
Base	1	180	115	25	Hardwood
Hinges	2	25			Brass Butt

23

JEWELLERY BOX

oxes for the safe keeping of jewellery have been around for centuries, and many have even been found in Ancient Egyptian tombs! The design has changed very little over the years but the materials used have changed considerably, often not for the better. Sadly, too many of the mass-produced boxes now available are so much alike – they all appear to be made from expensive timber, but the average buyer does not realise that liberal amounts of stain hide the poor quality below. A handmade box that is just a little different looks much better!

This box employs dovetail joints, but they are treated differently because the front and back slope outwards. Dovetails are intended to be used when adjoining sides meet at right angles, with both faces being upright. If the tails are marked out in the normal way for this box, the joint will be very weak and also look somewhat ridiculous. In this instance the tails should be marked out on the end pieces. They need to be marked from a right angle position and not from the sloping end; this is clearly shown in Fig 23.1.

METHOD

Select a suitable material for the carcase and plane it to size. Mark out the length of the front and back and cut to size. The ends need to be marked out, using a sliding bevel set to an angle of 75°, before cutting accurately to size (see Fig 23.2). Scribe a cutting line at the ends to the thickness of the front and back pieces. Mark the dimensions of the tails on the end grain of the end pieces with a sharp pencil, and square them across the thickness. Hold a square against the bottom edge and slide a dovetail template along the blade to mark out the tails.

Note that the front tails are different to those at the back (see Fig 23.3). Using a dovetail saw, cut down the pins and remove the waste between them. Transfer the dovetails to the ends of the

front and back, using a sharp scriber, and cut the pins. Dry-fit the joints and make any corrections needed; if you intend to fit a divider to the inside, now is the time to do it.

As the lid is curved and hinged by a pivot pin, the top edge of the back needs to be recessed into a curved shape to receive the corresponding shape of the lid. It is therefore best to leave the box at this stage and make the lid.

Select a suitable matching or contrasting piece of wood for this purpose, about 200mm × 145mm × 25mm. Plane the ends square and mark out the

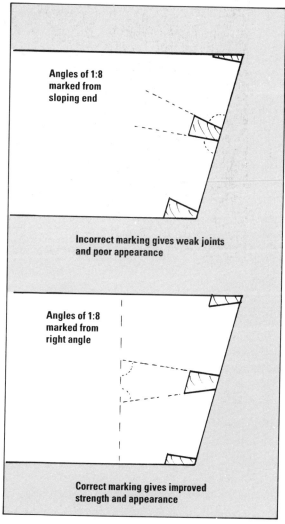

Angles of 1:8 marked from sloping end

Incorrect marking gives weak joints and poor appearance

Angles of 1:8 marked from right angle

Correct marking gives improved strength and appearance

Fig 23.1 Incorrect and correct dovetail marking.

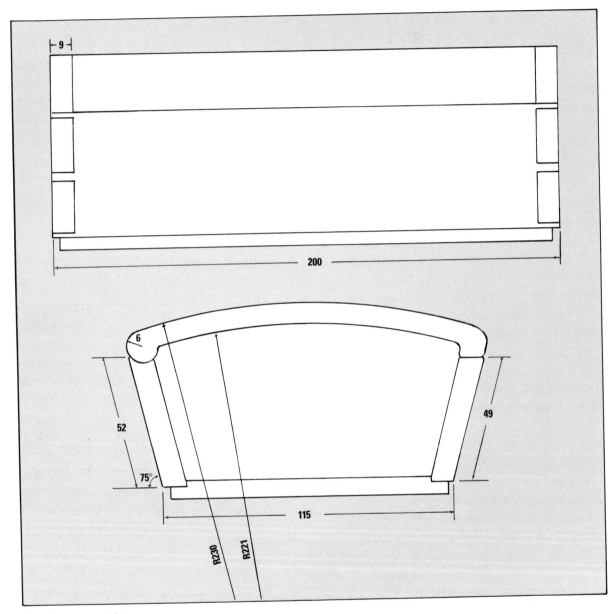

Fig 23.2 Front and end views.

required shape on them. It is worth making templates for both the outside and inside shapes, as these can be used to check your shaping throughout the stages.

Work the inside first by roughly removing as much waste as possible. Good old-fashioned wooden moulding planes are ideal for finishing at this stage; these planes can be obtained quite

cheaply even today, simply because so many were produced and very few of them are anything special. A half round plane of this type is ideal for shaping the rounding necessary on the back edge.

Continue to shape the outside to suit. When you are satisfied with the shape, mark out and cut the recess which will take the rounded back edge of the lid in the back of the box, using a router or a

Fig 23.3 Dovetail details.

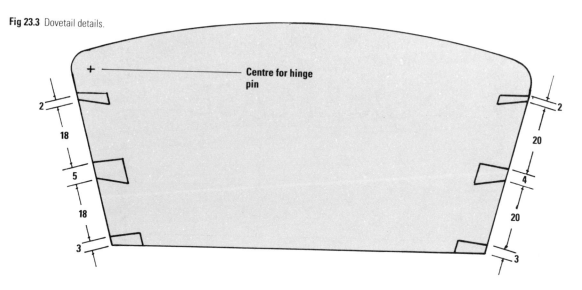

moulding plane. Clean up the inside of the box and assemble with care, leaving it cramped up until the glue has set.

Mark off the length of the lid and cut. Great care will be needed in planing the end grain; remember to work from each end, and do not plane right through. When the lid is fitted, the shape can be transferred to the ends and these can then be shaped to match.

Clean up the outside and mark the position of the hinge pivot: this pivot should be metal and about 3mm in diameter. Drill the holes through the ends and into the lid but slightly undersize. Open up the holes in the end pieces and into the lid – but only for most of the pivot's length – to the

full diameter needed. File a point on the inside ends of the pivot, but do not drive them in at this stage.

Select and prepare a base and cut a rebate around the edge to fit into the box. This will give a slight gap along the inside of the box, but should present no problem if you intend to line the inside. Should you not wish to do so, mitre the bottom edge of the dovetails and rebate the bottom of the box. Glue the base into the bottom of the box and allow the glue to set.

It is not possible to polish the lid after it has been fixed, so polish the box and the lid at this stage. Finally, drive the pivot into position and then line the box.

SUGGESTED CUTTING LIST					
Lengths are gross, widths and thicknesses are net. All measurements in millimetres					
PART	NO. REQUIRED	LENGTH	WIDTH	THICK	MATERIAL
Front	1	210	50	9	Hardwood
Back	1	210	50	9	Hardwood
Ends	2	150	75	9	Hardwood
Lid	1	200	145	25	Hardwood
Base	1	200	110	9	Hardwood
Pivot pins	2	20	3		Steel/brass
Divider	1	125	45	6	Hardwood

24

BRIEFCASE

Only a few years ago, no self-respecting schoolboy would arrive at school without a satchel; now only a briefcase will do! The Gladstone bag, named after the Prime Minister of the last century, was eventually developed into a type of briefcase. Nowadays there are various types of commercially produced case, some of which are very cheap in both price and quality. Many different materials are employed in the manufacture of briefcases, including aluminium, plastic, composition boards and leather. Although the range of sizes available is great, giving the purchaser a wide choice, it is much more satisfying to have a custom-built briefcase!

Make the case to suit your own purpose, both in size and the way that the inside is fitted out. A wooden case is likely to be quite heavy, so choose the timber with care. It needs to be strong and yet comparatively light in weight; chestnut is a good choice, but does tend to be a little soft. The case shown was made of vitex, which is hard, very strong and not too heavy. The lid and bottom were veneered with pomele, a name given to the blister figure sometimes displayed in mahogany.

The corner joints should ideally be dovetails, with the tails cut on the shorter sides so that when the case is being carried, the locking effect of the joints ensures that they do not pull apart. The locks and hinges can be found in old-fashioned leather repair shops, and should be fitted with bifurcated rivets. These are rivets that are forked at the end and are made in a variety of lengths and diameters. In use, the forks are bent at right angles to the main body of the rivet. I find that it is best to counterbore and bend the rivet over a washer set into the recess.

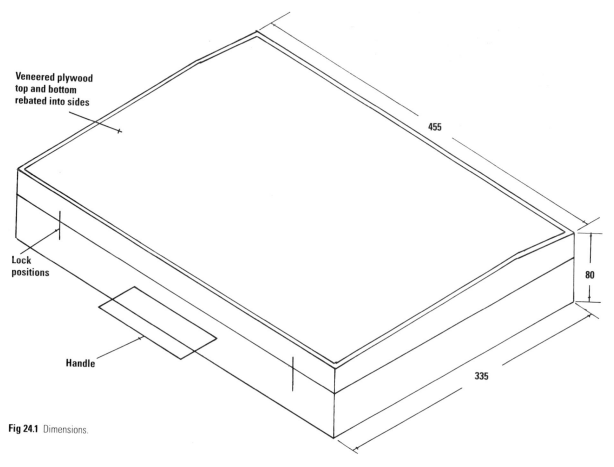

Veneered plywood
top and bottom
rebated into sides

455

Lock
positions

80

Handle

335

Fig 24.1 Dimensions.

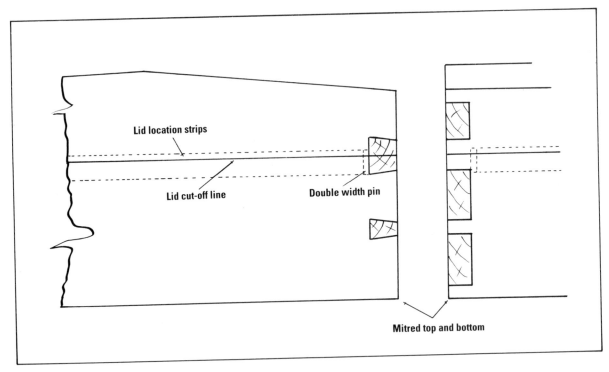

Fig 24.2 Dovetail details.

It is best to secure the handle with nuts and bolts, with the nuts recessed. To ensure that they do not work loose, one of two techniques can be used: either use two nuts tightened on to each other as locknuts, or apply a small amount of Loctite 601 or some similar adhesive.

METHOD

Select and prepare the timber to size and mark out the total length for each piece before cutting accurately (*see* Fig 24.1). Mark out the dovetails on the shorter pieces, remembering to mitre the top and bottom edges and to mark the pin double width for the cut-off lid. Cut the tails and the mitres and then set out the pins, using the tails as a template, before cutting them (*see* Fig 24.2).

Dry fit to check for accuracy before cutting the rebates at the top and bottom for the ply panels. (It is possible to cut the rebate after gluing up with a portable electric router. This will give rounded

end corners to the panels, which makes an interesting departure from the usual type of fitting.)

Glue up the carcase, taking care that the relatively thin material of the sides does not bend when cramped. While this is drying, the top and bottom can be prepared from 3mm plywood veneered with a suitable type of timber. The grain direction of the veneer needs to be thought about *before* it is cut! There will be no problem provided that the case is perfectly rectangular on its sides; however, if a double sloping top is used (as in the original), the grain of the ply must run along the longer length so that it can be 'bent' around the slopes.

Having ensured that the fit of the panels is satisfactory, glue them into position. If you want the double sloping top to follow the slopes over the entire width of the case, I recommend that one or two strengthening ribs are added. These should go from front to back, be the same shape as the

Fig 24.3 Rounded-off dovetails on the side.

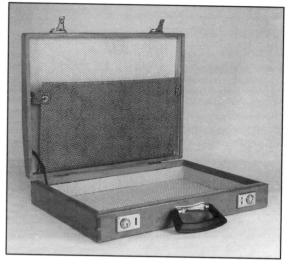

Fig 24.4 The lining and stay fitted.

ends and be jointed into the case front and back. Cramping up the panels without this arrangement will enable a concave curve surface to be formed.

The sides of the case can now be planed and all corners rounded off (*see* Fig 24.3). Mark the lid cut-off line with a marking gauge, cut to form the lid and clean up the cut surfaces. Paper will slide out between the lid and the case unless a strip is glued around the inside top edge of the case. Prepare strips of about 155mm × 3mm for this purpose, and cut mitres on the ends before gluing them in position.

Fit the hinges, locks and handle into their correct positions with wood screws; these are then removed to drill out the holes for the rivets and bolts. (Some types of lock will possibly need extra work, in the form of small blocks glued on to the case, to be able to work properly.)

Remove the hardware and polish the outside with a hard finish – oil for a dull surface, or Rustin's Clear Plastic Coating for a gloss or semi-matt finish. Line the insides with leather, refit the hardware and finally fit two stays to hold the lid in the open position (*see* Fig 24.4).

SUGGESTED CUTTING LIST					
Lengths are gross, widths and thicknesses are net. All measurements in millimetres					
PART	NO. REQUIRED	LENGTH	WIDTH	THICK	MATERIAL
Front/back	2	470	80	12	Hardwood
Sides	2	340	90	12	Hardwood
Lippings	2	440	15	3	Hardwood
Lippings	2	320	15	3	Hardwood
Locks	2				
Hinges	2				
Stays	2				
Pop studs	4				
Leather lining					

25
ELLIPTICAL AND CIRCULAR VENEER BOXES

The initial work for these two designs involves the same type of preparation and methods. It is only in the later stages that they become very different.

In both cases a mould needs to be made to the respective shape of the box. The sizes are unimportant, as is the shape of the ellipse – ellipses can be short and fat or long and thin, depending upon the major and minor axes. It is, however, important to note that the veneer must be able to bend around the 'pointed' end without splitting – and long rather than fat does look better! The mould can be made as described in Chapter 5 and finished smooth. If you make the mould for the circular box on a lathe, the side must be flat and not tapered at all.

The ellipse is not the easiest of shapes to construct, and geometry books explain about four different methods that can be used. By far the easiest to use is the trammel method shown in Fig 25.1: draw lines AB and CD at right angles to one another so that each is bisected by the other. These measurements will give the overall size of the box.

Make a trammel from a piece of stiff card or thin timber and mark points 1 and 2 from XC, i.e. half of the minor axis. Mark point 3 (from point 1) as the same size as AX. The trammel is moved so that point 2 is always on the major axis and point 3 always on the minor axis. The accuracy of the final ellipse will be considerably improved if a large number of marks are plotted.

A method that you will not find in any geometry book is of constructing an isometric circle with a pair of compasses (*see* Fig 25.2). It must be pointed out that this method is strictly *infra dig* and

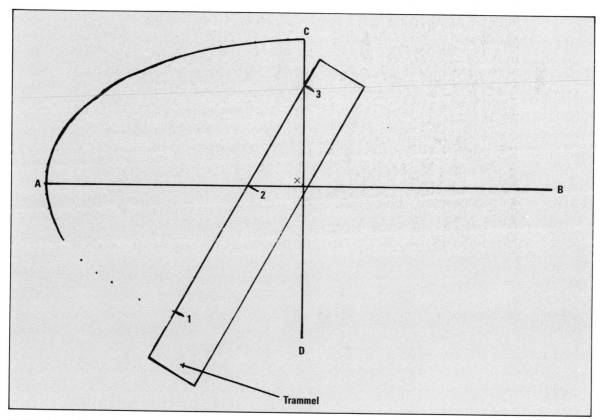

Fig 25.1 Constructing an ellipse with a trammel.

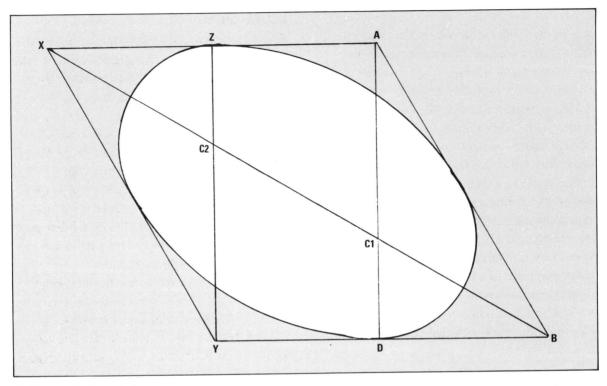

Fig 25.2 Isometric circle method.

inaccurate as far as geometry is concerned! When all is said and done, however, it is a useful and quick method, and will suffice for most occasions.

Construct an isometric square ABXY using angles of 30°. Draw AD and ZY at right angles to AX. Using a good quality pair of compasses, construct circles using C1 and C2 as the centres and C1D and C2Z as radii, followed by two more arcs with the radii of YZ and AD using Y and A as centres. If this is constructed on a suitable material, it can be used as the template for constructing the mould.

METHOD

Make a saw cut about 5mm in depth at a shallow angle across the side of the mould. This is needed to hold the end of the veneer steady when construction begins, so make sure that the saw produces a kerf wide enough to hold it. Polish the

mould with care to protect it from the glue that will soon be flying in all directions.

Each box requires one (2m–2.5m) length of veneer; cut the length to the required width plus a little for working. Slip one end of the veneer into the slot and bend it tightly around the mould until the length is totally wrapped. This ensures that you have a bit of practice without the glue, and will also give you an idea that the veneer is not going to split.

Repeat the operation, this time with glue: wrap the veneer until it reaches the holding point and mark the overlap position. Spread the glue on the remaining strip. *Do not* allow any glue to be on the initial layer, or you will only succeed in gluing the box to the mould!

Rewrap the veneer around the mould, pulling it tightly as you go, and finally cramp the veneer with plenty of tyre inner tube bands. It is essential that you now leave the box until the glue has totally cured. There is no hurry, so do not waste your time by removing the bands too early. The wood will absorb a certain amount of moisture from the glue, another reason for leaving the assembly until it is dry.

When the glue has cured, the mould can be pushed out of the inside with very little difficulty. Carefully lift the unglued veneer on the inside, feed in some glue and allow this to set. Although it probably will not need any cramping, it is a good idea to apply a little pressure by using a cramp and some shaped waste wood blocks, placing some paper between the block and the inside surface. When ready, carefully taper this end into the inside so that it appears as a flush surface.

Refit the box on to the mould so it stands proud by a small amount, and plane down until the edge is flat. Mark the width with a marking gauge and plane down to this line.

The final stage in this section of the work is to cautiously 'feather' in the end of the veneer on the outside. This is probably easiest if done with coarse glasspaper wrapped around a block; 80 grit will provide sufficient cutting power for this operation.

ELLIPTICAL BOX

Prepare from veneer a plywood for the top and the bottom; it will look good if the grain runs along the length of the box. Glasspaper the inside surfaces smooth and then glue them into position.

Cramp between two boards to provide even pressure with the cramps. When set, remove the overhanging waste using a spokeshave, finishing so you do not remove any of the box side.

Mark the line for the lid with a marking gauge. The position for this is quite critical, as too close to the top will be disastrous – the ply top will 'pull' the lid, creating a situation where it will not meet the box after a relatively short time.

A box as shown here will need the lid to be at least 15mm deep, and will be ideal if it is 18mm. Use a very fine saw and cut around the line. Smooth the two edges until the fit is perfect and then glue a location strip around the inside of the lid by wrapping veneer around in the same way as for the box. About two complete circuits will suffice.

Cramp until the glue has set, using ordinary clothes pegs. Trim this edge when the glue has cured. Finally, glasspaper the outside and polish.

SUGGESTED CUTTING LIST					
Lengths are gross, widths and thicknesses are net. All measurements in millimetres					
PART	NO. REQUIRED	LENGTH	WIDTH	THICK	MATERIAL
Sides	1	2500	50		Veneer
Top/bottom	10	210	110		Veneer
Location strip	1	1500	25		Veneer

26

CIRCULAR BOX

his box is divided into two separate boxes and therefore presents a greater challenge to the maker than others in this book. It is not harder to make *per se*, but it does demand considerable accuracy in construction.

The original idea came from a lesson that I was giving to a class, and illustrates a good point in design work. I was talking about the development of an idea and was using a sketch pad to illustrate the points being made (*see* Fig 26.1). Using an

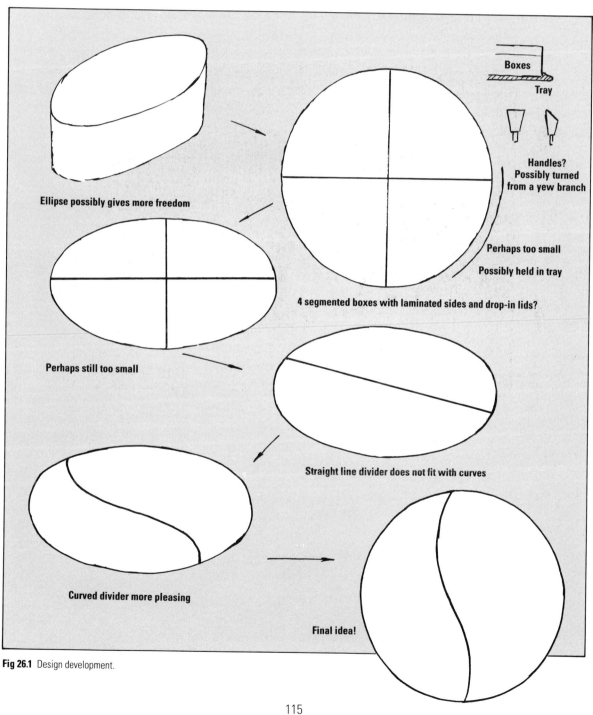

Ellipse possibly gives more freedom

Perhaps still too small

Curved divider more pleasing

Boxes

Tray

Handles? Possibly turned from a yew branch

Perhaps too small

Possibly held in tray

4 segmented boxes with laminated sides and drop-in lids?

Straight line divider does not fit with curves

Final idea!

Fig 26.1 Design development.

ellipse as the starting point (and unaware of the final outcome), I demonstrated that perhaps this shape could be divided into two separate boxes. This led to the possibility of dividing it up in different ways; perhaps a circle could be used.

Eventually I suggested that it could be divided by using a curved inside edge rather than a straight intersection. During the latter part of the discussion, a colleague arrived and stood listening until I was able to break off at a convenient point. He then said that he thought it was doubtful that this idea was workable. The class then insisted that I prove him wrong! Hence this box.

METHOD

When the circle has been made and the inside and outside veneers have been feathered, a two-part mould is needed for the dividers. Plan the curve accurately and transfer it to the mould material.

As two pieces are needed, the thickness of the two sets of veneers, together with a small allowance for saw cutting and cleaning up, should be marked out on the mould. Allow five layers of veneer for each part. This amount is removed from the mould and the two surfaces are smoothed up to mate accurately.

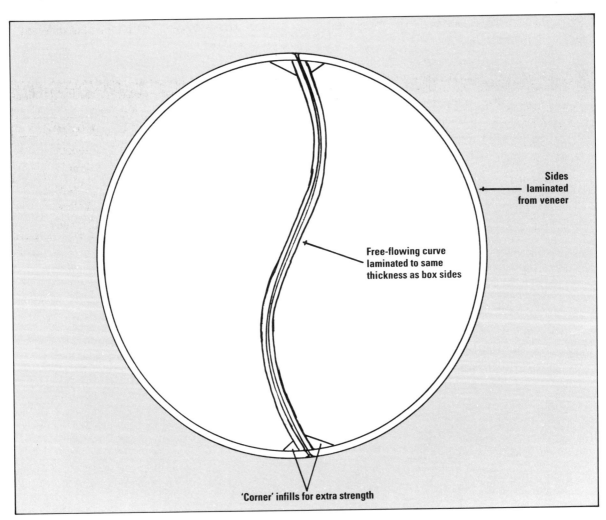

Sides laminated from veneer

Free-flowing curve laminated to same thickness as box sides

'Corner' infills for extra strength

Fig 26.2 Plan view.

Cut the veneer and glue the layers together, place them into the mould with a layer of paper on the outside surfaces and a thicker layer between the two, and cramp up. I have found that a layer of Pirelli webbing, or some similar material, is ideal for the divider in the mould. Allow the glue to cure before removing the cramps.

Mark the exact position for the two pieces and transfer these to the laminates. Cut them accurately and test in the box for fit. Remember, there must be a gap between the two pieces to allow for cutting with a fine back saw. When you are satisfied with the fit, glue the pieces into position. The 'corners' can be strengthened by the addition of small blocks shaped to fit; these are also glued in (see Fig 26.2).

Plane the top and bottom edges carefully before cutting the circle into the two pieces of boxes. Trim the cut ends accurately to the new inside ends, and then glue and cramp on a ply made from three layers of veneer. Try to arrange it so that the grain 'follows' from one box to the other. Trim back to the edges when the glue is set and mark out the lid depth, bearing in mind the 'pull' of the lid discussed in Chapter 25.

Location strips must be made and glued into the inside lid edges. The box is completed by the usual methods of cleaning up and polishing.

This technique can be used in many different way; lack of imagination is the big drawback for most of us, but it is well worth trying out different shapes and sizes.

SUGGESTED CUTTING LIST					
Lengths are gross, widths and thicknesses are net. All measurements in millimetres					
PART	NO. REQUIRED	LENGTH	WIDTH	THICK	MATERIAL
Sides	1	2500	50		Veneer
Divider sides	10	150	50		Veneer
Top/bottom	6	140	140		Veneer
Location	8	140	12		Veneer
Infills	4	50	10	7	Hardwood

27

EYE BOX

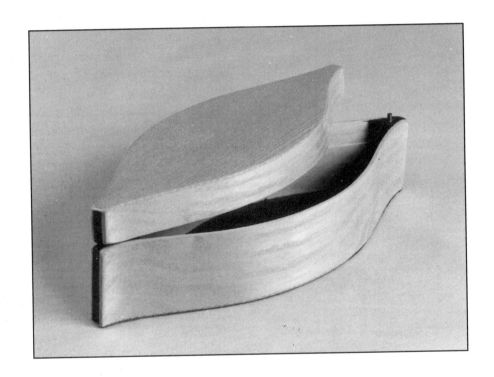

Designers are often enthused and influenced by their own individual likes. Occasionally a design comes because the eye has been drawn to something in a most unexpected manner. I remember Ted Hann, my first woodwork teacher, explaining how he was making a tea tray as part of his college course work. It had to include some form of decoration, and he was unable to think of anything suitable. He and some friends went to the 'pictures' (as the cinema was then called), and suddenly on the screen was an aerial view of a team of formation dancers. Here was his inspiration!

I find that nature provides the ideas and impetus so frequently, and this box is no exception. When I embarked on the making of veneer boxes, it quickly became obvious that shapes of infinite variety were possible. The problem, as always, is inspiration, but in the case of this box it was with me and right in front of me every day!

METHOD

The mould must come first – see Chapter 5 for details. Mark out a template for one side of the box (see Fig 27.1), making the necessary allowance for the router guide bush. As the box is to be made from five layers of veneer, a 5mm cutter is ideal, so include this in your calculations. Cut the template to shape, adjust where necessary and smooth the edges with abrasive paper. Remember, this template must be 100% precise if the mould is to stand any chance of being accurate.

Cut sufficient MDF pieces to the same size to give a mould size of about 75mm, and fix the template to each piece in turn. Using a 5mm straight flute cutter, cut through each piece in turn and then glue the pieces together to form the two parts of the mould. If this is done carefully, very little work will be needed and the mould can be smoothed and polished.

Select your veneer and cut 10 strips approximately 300mm × 70mm; as you are not producing real plywood, the grain will run along the length on all pieces. Choose which pieces will be on the outsides and insides, and mark them accordingly.

Spread glue thinly and evenly as needed before cramping in the mould, making sure that you protect the mould with a few layers of paper. Leave the laminates until the glue has hardened fully; there is no benefit in uncramping too early, so be patient! The entire process is then repeated for the other side.

Meanwhile, the top and bottom sheets can be glued up, using three layers of veneer. The difference here is that you must make up a proper plywood by ensuring that the grain of the middle laminate is at right angles to those adjacent to it.

When the sides are thoroughly dry, plane the top edge of each side with a block plane, then mark the width with a marking gauge to 65mm and plane to the line. As it is difficult to hold in this state, cramp the side into the mould in the bench vice. Mark off the length on each side, square a line and saw off most of the waste, leaving a small allowance at each end.

Select the wood for the two end infills with the grain running along the 22mm length. Working on such small pieces can be very difficult, so, to help maintain an even temper, keep the piece long and work on the two ends of it for these pieces. Shape them so they fit well between the two sides, and only then cut them to length.

Glasspaper the insides of the front and back pieces, together with the inside ends of the infills, and then glue together (see Fig 27.1). Provided you have a good fit, very little pressure will be needed from cramps. Level the bottom edge when the glue has set, and then glue on the bottom laminates after the inside surface has been sanded smooth. It is best to cramp this on between two boards to ensure equal pressure.

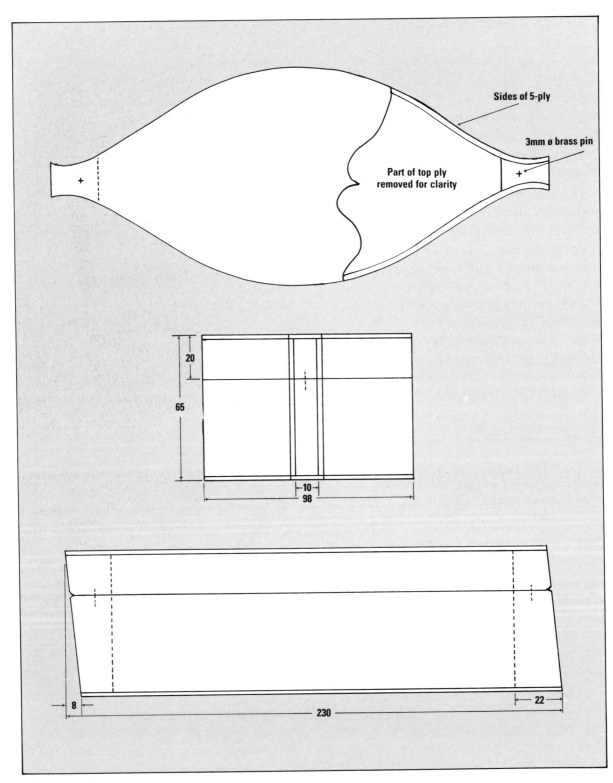

Fig 27.1 Front, end and plan views.

When ready, remove the cramps and level the top edge, but do not fix the top laminate yet. Mark out the position of the two location pins and drill vertically, using a 3mm bit, to a depth of 25mm (*see* Fig 27.2). Drilling at this stage saves hassle later! The top laminate can now be glued on in the same way as for the bottom.

Remove the bulk of the overhanging top and bottom and then use a spokeshave and abrasive paper to finish off. Mark out the tapering ends, saw to the waste side of the line and plane to the line with a finely set block plane.

Using a marking gauge, scribe a line 20mm from the top and then, using as fine a saw as possible, cut around to separate the lid. The two exposed edges can then be smoothed and the ends rounded down as shown in Fig 27.1, before the brass location pins are cut and glued into the bottom section. Finally, glasspaper the box and polish.

For those who want a bit more excitement and challenge, why not inlay veneer in the form of an eyeball into the top?

Fig 27.2 The locating pin in place.

SUGGESTED CUTTING LIST					
Lengths are gross, widths and thicknesses are net. All measurements in millimetres					
PART	**NO. REQUIRED**	**LENGTH**	**WIDTH**	**THICK**	**MATERIAL**
Sides	10	260	70		Veneer
Top/bottom	6	230	100		Veneer
Infills	2	25	60	20	Hardwood
Location pins	2	10	3		Brass

28

HEART BOX

In many respects, this box is very similar in construction to the Eye box (*see* Chapter 27), the main difference being in the mould, which might need to be a three-part construction. This will depend entirely on the shape that is selected for each side of the heart, but the box can be made with a straightforward two-part mould. It all depends on whether the mould can be assembled easily when the veneer is being held – sometimes this is impossible, and a more complex three-part mould will be needed. As always, the mould must be accurate, so take care in its construction.

I have made this box in a variety of timbers, sometimes using contrasting timbers and at other times making entirely from one type of wood. The choice is yours, but select a variety which will complement the design.

METHOD

Cut five strips of veneer per side to the depth of the finished box plus an allowance of about 6mm for wastage. Coat the veneer with glue and cramp into the mould, with layers of paper protecting it from glue. This will need to be repeated for the other side of the heart.

When both sides have been completed, plane the base edges flat, then gauge the required width and plane them to width. The top of the heart is joined by a butt joint, but the bottom uses an infill piece as described in Chapter 26 and shown in Fig 28.1: this can be of the same material, or can contrast with the main box timber.

When satisfied with the fit at each end, clean up the inside surfaces and then assemble with glue. Try a dry run first, especially to make sure that you know which cramps to use and how to use them!

The top and bottom are constructed from a handmade plywood of three veneers. When these are ready, mark out the shape required and cut them out, making sure that you leave plenty of waste. Glasspaper the inside surfaces and then glue them on to the box sides. Shape back to the sides, using spokeshaves and glasspaper.

Mark the lid cut-off line around the box, and cut on the line with a fine saw. Smooth the mating edges and then prepare two strips made from two veneers. These are then glued around the inside of the lid and act as locators for the lid.

The inside can be lined with a suitable material or left in its natural state. Finally, clean up the outside and polish.

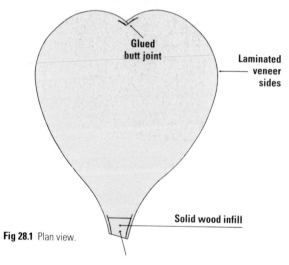

Fig 28.1 Plan view.

SUGGESTED CUTTING LIST					
Lengths are gross, widths and thicknesses are net. All measurements in millimetres					
PART	NO. REQUIRED	LENGTH	WIDTH	THICK	MATERIAL
Sides	10	250	50		Veneer
Top/bottom	6	180	150		Veneer
Infill	1	20	45	15	Hardwood
Locations	4	250	10		Veneer

29

A CELEBRATION OF WOOD

As a result of being taught by a man whose love of timber was infectious, I too developed a great love for this tremendous material; this resulted in my reading books about timber as other people read novels, and I then began to collect samples of timber. When I was teaching GCE A level students this collection was a teaching resource, but it has grown just like Topsy – and most collections! The timber has been confined to cardboard boxes in my workshop for far too long now, and the time has come to house it in a fitting environment.

A box of this nature has to celebrate the beauty of its contents, but must not be so elaborate that it becomes pretentious. I have made this box to suit my ideas and for part of my collection, so I have been somewhat restrained in its decoration. This is very much an individual thing, and is a classic example of when a design should not be slavishly imitated.

As the purpose is celebration, I decided that the only way to produce such a box was to use the ultimate in joints, and so it is designed to be made using the mitred secret dovetail. I also wanted a rich look to the box, and I decided to use a block of padauk from the Andaman Islands for the carcase. This wood has been sitting in my workshop for years, just waiting for something special – it was given me by an old craftsman, who had kept it for over 40 years. The base is veneered in Indian rosewood, and the top is quartered English oak inlaid with snakewood.

The box had to be simple in shape, but at the same time it had to be different and striking; this resulted in the use of curves cut into the sides on a bevel system.

The size of the individual samples has to be established early on. I found that I had to compromise on this, and in the end 65mm × 50mm became the standard size. Make sure that the samples are not packed too tightly, otherwise you will not be able to remove them.

METHOD

Begin by carefully selecting your timber for the carcase and plane it to size (*see* Fig 29.1). If you decide to use mitred secret dovetails, cut all pieces to the exact length required and follow the instructions provided in Chapter 3. Make sure that you clearly mark the top edges; when the box is cut for the lid, it is essential that you cut through a double width pin – and nowhere else! Remember that when this joint is glued, without accurate labelling, you have no reference point to see.

Having cut the joints and dry-assembled them, mark the position of the dividers. These need to be housed in, but not to their full width.

Mark the thickness of the divider with a sharp knife and a square, and its width and depth with a marking gauge. The same settings need to be marked on each divider. The housings can be cut with an electric router or by hand. When by hand, chop out a recess at the closed end of the housing and then use a saw to cut down to the depth before removing the waste with a chisel (*see* Fig 29.2). Cut out the small section of waste on the ends of each divider and try for fit (*see* Fig 29.3).

Work rebates for the top and bottom around the top and bottom edges. Clean up and polish all inside surfaces before gluing the box together, including the dividers.

Prepare and fit the bottom panel and glue it in. The top should be rebated before fitting, especially if you intend to work a similar type of decoration to that shown.

When the top has been fixed into place, the grooves for decoration can be cut and filled with your choice of material. The cut-off lid can now be marked out. Work any decorative shaping at this point before cleaning up the outside surfaces; then cut off the lid and clean up the cut lines before fitting the brass butt hinges.

Prepare a lid lifter type of handle, using yet another type of timber; this can be for the full

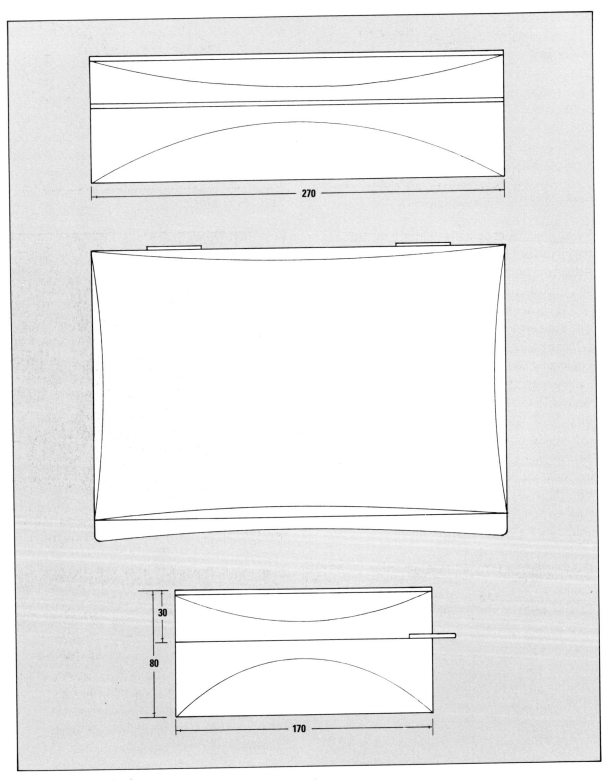

Fig 29.1 Front, end and plan views.

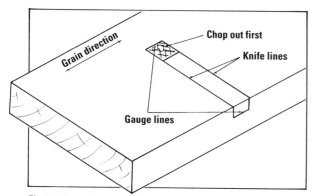

Fig 29.2 Removing waste wood.

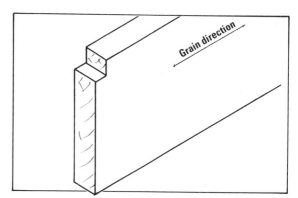

Fig 29.3 Divider end detail.

length of the front or much shorter. If the latter, the lid can be placed centrally or towards one end. Rebate the front edge to receive this, and shape and clean it up before gluing into position.

Finally, the box should be polished and packed with the samples.

Having selected the samples, prepare a catalogue to be fixed to the inside of the lid so that each timber is labelled and can be identified easily. (This will be an easy task for those who have access to a word processor; these fortunate individuals could further improve their collection by preparing a database on which full details can be stored and retrieved when needed.) Prepare a suitable holder to keep the list safely and in position in the lid, using another timber for this holder (*see* Fig 29.4).

Fig 29.4 The index leaflet and its holder, and the divisions in the body.

SUGGESTED CUTTING LIST					
Lengths are gross, widths and thicknesses are net. All measurements in millimetres					
PART	**NO. REQUIRED**	**LENGTH**	**WIDTH**	**THICK**	**MATERIAL**
Front/back	2	280	75	15	Hardwood
Ends	2	175	75	15	Hardwood
Top	1	280	175	7	Hardwood
Base	1	280	175	3	Plywood
Dividers	3	150	35	4	Hardwood
Hinges	2	25			Brass butt
Sundry material for decoration					

GLOSSARY

Aliphatic glue Modern, water- and heat-resistant white liquid glue. Requires relatively short cramping times.

Aluminium oxide Self-lubricating and long-lasting type of abrasive paper.

Animal glue Made from the bones and hides of animals, this needs to be used hot. Not water- or heatproof.

Back saw Any member of the saw family whose blade is strengthened by a strip of metal along its top edge.

Block plane A small metal plane, ideally suited for the planing of end grain. The blade is set at an angle of either 12° or 18°. The mouth is often adjustable.

Burr Abnormal, wort-like growth, found on many types of tree. The burr is a mass of dense tissue that is contorted and interwoven. Very decorative and prized for veneer.

Butt hinge Hinge made of steel or brass, sunk into the timber. Both halves are of the same width and rectangular.

Butt joint Simple joint where two pieces of wood are held together by glue or panel pins only.

Chamfer A bevel of 45° worked on edges and corners.

Chipboard A man-made sheet material, made by gluing chips of wood together and compressing them under high pressure.

Coping saw A member of the frame saw family, using a throwaway blade. Ideal for the removal of waste in dovetail joints and for cutting curves.

Countersink A conical depression cut to receive a countersunk screw head, enabling the head to be flush with or below the surface of the material.

Cutting gauge Similar to a marking gauge but with a knife-type blade instead of a spur. Used only across the grain and parallel to an edge.

Cyanoacrylate Modern chemical adhesive which sets in seconds (also known as superglue). Needs great care in use, as skin can be bonded as well as the material!

Danish oil A drying oil, based on tung oil, with the addition of other vegetable oils and resins. Good penetration properties.

Dovetail joints A corner joint where one part resembles a dove's tail and the other part has pins which fit into the gaps between the tails. There are several types including common, lap and mitred secret dovetail joints.

Dovetail saw A member of the back saw family having fine teeth of at least 14 teeth per 25mm.

Dovetail template Device (generally home-made) to assist in the marking out of dovetail joints.

Face side The best side of a piece of wood, planed first and accurately flat, straight and without twist. Marking-out operations are made from this side.

Face edge The best edge, planed after the face side and similarly flat, straight, without twist and at 90° to the face side.

Garnet paper Long-lasting abrasive paper with a good cutting action.

Glasspaper Abrasive paper made from ground glass.

Glue film A film of glue that is bonded to a release paper and sold in sheets. Used for laying veneer, it needs the use of a domestic electric iron to provide heat to melt the glue.

Groove A narrow channel, generally square or rectangular, which is cut to receive a panel.

Hardwood Timber that comes from broad-leaved deciduous or evergreen trees, or dicotyledons. The term does not imply that the wood is hard; indeed, the softest hardwood commercially available is softer than any of the softwoods.

***Ikedame* saw** A fine cutting Japanese back saw, which cuts on the pull stroke.

Jack plane Bench plane used for the initial preparation of timber to size.

Kerf A saw groove the width of the saw.

Keys A veneer or thicker piece of timber set into a mitre joint to increase strength. Often used as a decorative feature.

Laminate A single layer used to build up a thicker material, as in plywood.

Linseed oil A slow-drying oil made from the seed of the flax plant. Now superseded to a large extent by other oils.

Marking gauge A tool used for marking lines along the grain, parallel to an edge.

Medium density fibreboard (MDF) A man-made board of various thicknesses, available in sheet form. Very stable, it can be shaped with hand and machine tools.

Mitre joint Generally used as a corner joint, but without a great deal of strength. The joint bisects the intersection of the two pieces.

Mitre square A tool used for the accurate marking of 45°.

Plough plane A hand plane especially made for the cutting of grooves of various sizes.

Plywood A man-made board material made from several layers of veneer. Each layer, or laminate, is glued to its neighbour, with the grain of each piece at 90° alternately. This produces a very strong material.

Polyvinyl acetate (PVA) A modern, ready-to-use, white liquid glue, which is relatively quick-setting.

Rebate A square or rectangular recess cut on the edge of a piece of timber, generally to receive a plywood panel or a door.

Rebate plane A specially made plane for cutting rebates.

Router There are two types: a special plane (once known as 'the old woman's tooth'!) for levelling the bottom of grooves, now seldom used, and the electric router. This portable machine can replace many hand operations such as rebating, grooving and producing mouldings.

Sanding sealer A shellac- or cellulose-based liquid for sealing grain prior to applying other types of finish. (Cellulose-based sealers must be used in a well-ventilated area, away from naked flames.)

Scriber A sharp and long pointed tool steel rod used in marking out joints.

Shoulder plane A precision-made narrow plane with the side faces machined at right angles to the sole, principally for working on end grain shoulders in some joints, such as the secret mitre dovetail. The blade is set at a low angle.

Sliding bevel A tool which can be set to any angle, for marking out or testing purposes.

Smoothing plane A bench plane similar to the jack plane but much shorter in length. Used for the final cleaning-up of wood prior to the use of scrapers and abrasive papers.

Softwood Woods obtained from trees that have needle-shaped leaves and are generally coniferous gymnosperms. Softwood is a botanical description, and does not refer to the hardness of the timber.

Strap hinge Similar to a butt hinge, but much longer and narrower.

Teak oil A drying oil based on tung oil, teak oil is easy to use, giving a sheen and good protection to the timber.

Tenon saw General purpose saw from the back saw family.

Try-square A tool for testing for squareness and for marking out lines at right angles to a side.

Tung oil Slow-drying, natural vegetable oil from China.

Urea formaldehyde Water- and heat-resistant chemical glue which requires a hardener to begin the chemical setting.

Veneer Very thin sheets of timber cut from the log in a variety of ways, used to cover a cheap base material with exotic timbers.

SUPPLIERS

KEY   **V** Veneer
T Tools   **H** Hardware
WN UK native wood   **P** Polish
WE Exotic Wood   **S** Sundries

The Art Veneers Company Ltd
Chiswick Avenue Industrial Estate
Mildenhall
Suffolk IP28 7AY
V, T, H

John Boddy's
Riverside Sawmills
Boroughbridge
N. Yorks YO5 9LJ
T, WN, WE, V, H, S

The Working Tree
Milland Fine Timber Ltd
Milland
Nr. Liphook
Hants GU30 7JS
WN, WE (*from managed sources*)

Rustin's Ltd
Waterloo Road
Cricklewood
London NW2 7TX
P (*including oils and polishing sundries*)

Mackintosh Craft Woods
Unit 7
Fort Fareham
Newgate Lane
Fareham PO14 IAH
WN, WE, P

Robert Bosch Ltd
PO Box 98
Broadwater Park
North Orbital Road
Denham
Uxbridge UB9 5HJ
Routers and electrical hand tools

Richard Sarjent
116 Manchester Road
Swindon SN1 2AF
Japanese chisels, **T, P,** *machinery*

CRM Saw Company Ltd
17 Arnside Road
Waterlooville PO7 7UP
Machinery, power tools, saw sharpening

BriMarc Associates
Unit 8 Ladbrooke Park
Millers Road
Warwick CV34 5AE
T, H, S *and Speed Frame Cramp*

INDEX

METRIC CONVERSION TABLE

INCHES TO MILLIMETRES AND CENTIMETRES					
MM = Millimetres CM = Centimetres					
INCHES	**MM**	**CM**	**INCHES**	**CM**	**INCHES**	**CM**
⅛	3	0.3	9	22.9	30	76.2
¼	6	0.6	10	25.4	31	78.7
⅜	10	1.0	11	27.9	32	81.3
½	13	1.3	12	30.5	33	83.8
⅝	16	1.6	13	33.0	34	86.4
¾	19	1.9	14	35.6	35	88.9
⅞	22	2.2	15	38.1	36	91.4
1	25	2.5	16	40.6	37	94.0
1¼	32	3.2	17	43.2	38	96.5
1½	38	3.8	18	45.7	39	99.1
1¾	44	4.4	19	48.3	40	101.6
2	51	5.1	20	50.8	41	104.1
2½	64	6.4	21	53.3	42	106.7
3	76	7.6	22	55.9	43	109.2
3½	89	8.9	23	58.4	44	111.8
4	102	10.2	24	61.0	45	114.3
4½	114	11.4	25	63.5	46	116.8
5	127	12.7	26	66.0	47	119.4
6	152	15.2	27	68.6	48	121.9
7	178	17.8	28	71.1	49	124.5
8	203	20.3	29	73.7	50	127.0

ABOUT THE AUTHOR

PHOTOGRAPH BY DEREK COOPER

JOHN BENNETT was born in Romsey, Hampshire, and educated mainly in Southampton. He qualified as a teacher from Shoreditch Training College and taught woodwork, metalwork, technical drawing and design at both grammar and comprehensive schools as well as in recreational further education classes.

His great love for, and knowledge of, wood has featured strongly in his life. He is well known as a craftsman, in particular for church commissions, when he has frequently been called upon to design and make crosses and other church furniture.

After 30 years in the classroom, he was forced into early retirement on health grounds, which enabled him to gain much satisfaction from working with and writing about the subject he loves most – wood. He is married, with three grown-up children, and lives in Hampshire.

TITLES AVAILABLE FROM
GMC PUBLICATIONS LTD

BOOKS

Woodworking Plans and Projects	GMC Publications
40 More Woodworking Plans and Projects	GMC Publications
Woodworking Crafts Annual	GMC Publications
Woodworkers' Career and Educational Source Book	GMC Publications
Woodworkers' Courses and Source Book	GMC Publications
Useful Woodturning Projects	GMC Publications
Woodturning Techniques	GMC Publications
Green Woodwork	Mike Abbott
Furniture Restoration and Repair for Beginners	Kevin Jan Bonner
Woodturning Jewellery	Hilary Bowen
The Incredible Router	Jeremy Broun
Electric Woodwork	Jeremy Broun
Woodcarving: A Complete Course	Ron Butterfield
Making Fine Furniture: Projects	Tom Darby
Restoring Rocking Horses	Clive Green and Anthony Dew
Heraldic Miniature Knights	Peter Greenhill
Practical Crafts: Seat Weaving	Ricky Holdstock
Multi-centre Woodturning	Ray Hopper
Complete Woodfinishing	Ian Hosker
Woodturning: A Source Book of Shapes	John Hunnex
Making Shaker Furniture	Barry Jackson
Upholstery: A Complete Course	David James
Upholstery Techniques and Projects	David James
The Upholsterer's Pocket Reference Book	David James
Designing and Making Wooden Toys	Terry Kelly

Making Dolls' House Furniture	Patricia King
Making and Modifying Woodworking Tools	Jim Kingshott
The Workshop	Jim Kingshott
Sharpening: The Complete Guide	Jim Kingshott
Turning Wooden Toys	Terry Lawrence
Making Board, Peg and Dice Games	Jeff and Jennie Loader
Making Wooden Toys and Games	Jeff and Jennie Loader
The Complete Dolls' House Book	Jean Nisbett
The Secrets of the Dolls' House Makers	Jean Nisbett
Wildfowl Carving, Volume 1	Jim Pearce
Make Money from Woodturning	Ann and Bob Phillips
Guide to Marketing	Jack Pigden
Woodcarving Tools, Materials and Equipment	Chris Pye
Making Tudor Dolls' Houses	Derek Rowbottom
Making Georgian Dolls' Houses	Derek Rowbottom
Making Period Dolls' House Furniture	Derek and Sheila Rowbottom
Woodturning: A Foundation Course	Keith Rowley
Turning Miniatures in Wood	John Sainsbury
Pleasure and Profit from Woodturning	Reg Sherwin
Making Unusual Miniatures	Graham Spalding
Woodturning Wizardry	David Springett
Adventures in Woodturning	David Springett
Furniture Projects	Rod Wales
Decorative Woodcarving	Jeremy Williams

VIDEOS

Dennis White Teaches Woodturning:	
Part 1	Turning Between Centres
Part 2	Turning Bowls
Part 3	Boxes, Goblets and Screw Threads
Part 4	Novelties and Projects
Part 5	Classic Profiles
Part 6	Twists and Advanced Turning
Ray Gonzalez	Carving a Figure: The Female Form

Jim Kingshott	Sharpening the Professional Way
Jim Kingshott	Sharpening, Turning and Carving Tools
David James	The Traditional Upholstery Workshop Part 1: Stuffover Upholstery
David James	The Traditional Upholstery Workshop Part 2: Drop-in and Pinstuffed Seats
John Jordan	Bowl Turning
John Jordan	Hollow Turning

MAGAZINES

Woodcarving   Woodturning   Businessmatters

GMC Publications regularly produces new books and videos on a wide range of woodworking and craft subjects, and an increasing number of specialist magazines, all available on subscription:

All these publications are available through bookshops and newsagents, or may be ordered by post from the publishers at 166 High Street, Lewes, East Sussex BN7 1XU, telephone (01273) 477374, fax (01273) 478606. Credit card orders are accepted.

PLEASE WRITE OR PHONE FOR A FREE CATALOGUE